Lorraine Cavanagh is an Anglican priest in the Church in Wales, and was the Anglican chaplain to Cardiff University. She is the author of *The Really Useful Meditation Book* (2004) and *By One Spirit: Reconciliation and Renewal in Anglican Life* (2009).

MAKING SENSE OF GOD'S LOVE

Atonement and Redemption

LORRAINE CAVANAGH

First published in Great Britain in 2011

Society for Promoting Christian Knowledge
36 Causton Street
London SW1P 4ST
www.spckpublishing.co.uk

British Library Cataloguing-in-Publication Data
A catalogue record for this book is available from the British Library

ISBN 978–0–281–06403–8

1 3 5 7 9 10 8 6 4 2

Typeset by Graphicraft Ltd, Hong Kong
Manufacture managed by Jellyfish
Printed in Great Britain by CPI

Produced on paper from sustainable forests

For Alys

Contents

Introduction

This book is one of the first in the Modern Church 'Making Sense of Christianity' series. As with the rest of the series, it aims to promote a liberal and compassionate approach to its subject. There are many people who are put off Christianity by the way the doctrines of atonement and redemption are communicated. People find it hard to believe in a loving God who appears at the same time to be so angry and vindictive. Many of them also feel that the things Christians teach, publicly or privately, do not connect with them in any meaningful way. This is either because they are put off by the narrow theological framework in which Christianity is often presented, or because what is said about atonement and redemption seems highly theoretical and remote from their experience of life as it really is. The book therefore seeks to address some of the difficult questions that these people are asking. It is also written for those who may be wanting to return to their faith, or who would like to explore it in greater depth or in a more open theological landscape, having perhaps suffered personally as a result of too great an emphasis being placed on the penal substitutionary theory of atonement. My hope is that they will all find in this book a new understanding of what it really means to live as people who have been forgiven and brought home into a more honest and deeper relationship with God through the atoning and redemptive work of Jesus Christ.

Part 1

MAKING SENSE OF ATONEMENT

1

Why atonement?

Why do we need atonement? Why is God so violent? Why did Christ have to die? Doesn't the Church need to atone for its own past? How do we connect with atonement today?

No matter how hard they try, human beings cannot hide from the past. Neither can they avoid taking responsibility for history in the present. Global conflicts from the Middle East to the Balkan States, and from Africa to Northern Ireland, have shown that it is impossible for any one generation to opt out of the ongoing events which make their history by attempting to forget without having first forgiven. Without an ongoing and truthful forgiveness, the past returns in violent episodic attempts to shift the burden of blame on to the other person or group.

'To begin to live in the present, we must first atone for our past, and be finished with it . . .'[1] These words from Chekhov's *The Cherry Orchard* express an underlying human anxiety about blame. Blame and responsibility for suffering are either assumed to belong together or are confused with each other, so that someone or something must be blamed, or held responsible, if suffering is to be at all bearable. But blaming the other makes a victim of both. There is very little one party can do when blamed for the cause of a dispute, except to pass the blame back to another person or to an earlier event, or bring it forward into the present by transferring it to a group or individual involved in the current conflict situation. Bringing it forward into the present widens the circle of violence and feeds into the existing stagnant pool of distrust and recrimination which, so far, has failed to sustain the common life or give hope for the future. The Cold War years were an example of the kind of sterile and static climate of fear in which a war that was in every sense cold was sustained. Unlike blame, taking responsibility for the suffering caused to another involves an active, or dynamic, initiative. It moves the situation forward and allows for the possibility of a future by involving the active engagement of one or both parties with the pain which has been caused. Where blame looks for a passive victim, taking responsibility works in a common will for active reconciliation which will in turn sustain the renewed life of a future community or relationship.

Chekhov was writing towards the end of the nineteenth century when psychology was still in its infancy. There were few acceptable ways of explaining and attempting to address feelings of personal guilt or of a shared sense of historical responsibility for the actions of previous generations. Despite this, the need to make up for past actions and events has figured in our emotional landscape for as long as human beings have been able to record their story. Art dating from the earliest millennia seems to link sacrifice with the need to atone for something in placating a wrathful god. In the early part of the twentieth century Jung connected the subconscious and dreams with the conscious thoughts and feelings of his patients. At the same time, he allowed his thinking to be informed by the spiritual dimension of the human psyche and with the way in which paying attention to the shadow side of human personality helps us come to terms with guilt. Jung's understanding of the spiritual was also shaped by an understanding of a higher power which embodied both dark and light, good and bad.

Alienation and blame – on not being a loser

The idea of atoning for past actions implies a human need for the kind of relatedness which comes with forgiveness, when the bond of trust is re-established and a person no longer feels alone or alienated. Alone, we cannot bear ourselves, or the harsh realities which confront us daily in the news. But, at the same time, we are accustomed to them and to having to live at times in a state of chronic loneliness. Human beings have learned to adapt to violence and pain by putting up defences which separate, or alienate, them from each other. Violence and pain are also deeply embedded in our unconscious or inner world, and we accept the fact that most people, as well as whole nations and communities, experience alienation at some point in their individual lives or in their history.

Alienation, as it is defined from the word 'alienate', is a sense of 'isolation or estrangement' from others.[2] Violent crimes such as those witnessed in Hungerford in 1987, Dunblane in 1996 and, more recently in 2010, on a single day in a number of small villages in Cumbria, suggest that alienation is part of even the most apparently 'normal' person's emotional constitution. While it does not usually result in multiple killings, for most of us alienation amounts to what Jesus would have called 'hardness of heart'. It is part of a technique for surviving and succeeding in a hard world. To be a 'loser' is to be 'soft', and a soft person becomes a soft target, someone who cannot survive, who cannot fight their patch and who is therefore a natural victim.[3] War, massacres and crime on the streets are the result of alienation caused by the human capacity to inflict damage on ourselves and on our surroundings. It requires that we continually review and revise the language we use to explain evil and the Christian understanding of atonement.

In the world and in people's lives, things have gone wrong. Decisions have been taken and choices made for all the wrong reasons. Sometimes we sense, from having lived with the consequences of these errors of choice and judgement, that we lack something, that we live in a state of estrangement with regard to the kind of relationship that fills the gap which work and lifestyle cannot fill. Alienation brings with it a sense of a particular friendship having been spoiled, even if the friendship has carried on without the shared

Alienation brings a sense of a particular friendship having been spoiled

pain or disappointment ever being mentioned, let alone resolved. This suggests that, through the spoiling of human relationships, there is a greater relationship which needs to be put right.

Coming to terms with reality

In his poem 'The Hound of Heaven' Francis Thompson speaks of the way denial of this particular relationship, and of the need to put it right, affects our perspective on happiness and our sense of self-worth. In spoiling this unique relationship we have wounded ourselves, so that our actions and choices become a form of self-betrayal, a denial of our true self and of the good in us which can only be re-created in relationship with the God who is Love itself. 'All things betray thee, who betrayest Me.'[4]

We know ourselves to be relating beings and that our attempts at relationship go wrong because of our human nature and its inclination for destroying the people and things we need most. But this self-awareness is also a sign of maturity and of a coming to terms with reality itself. It begins to make reality 'bearable'. Knowing who we are and what we lack is grounded in something which has to do with realizing the full implication of what it means to be human and the effect human nature has on our attempts to relate to others, including the physical world and those with whom we share it. Right relationship with the higher power which we call God is worked out in all other relationships, although this productive working can only take effect when both parties, God and human beings, are working towards the same ends, the purposes of a loving God for *all* people, and not only for one group or one individual. The paradox lies in finding success in understanding ourselves as responsible beings acting within this wider loving purpose, if we are to truly 'succeed' in our individual lives. Chekhov's words therefore speak of something more than drawing a line under the past, or a veil over past wrongs.

> **Our attempts at relationship go wrong because of our inclination for destroying the people and things we need most**

Reconnecting with the past

Atoning for the past is about reconnecting the past with the present. In other words, it allows for a healing of the past in facing the pain which it caused and which is still being experienced in the present. One of the most recent examples of healing and atonement on a national scale was effected through the South African Truth and Reconciliation Commission, mediated by Archbishop Desmond

Tutu. It revealed atonement to be a process of reparation, like the mending of a torn fabric. This kind of atonement process does not try to pretend that the damage never happened. Instead, a new creation emerges out of the damage itself, so that what has 'gone wrong' is 'put right' in bringing past and present together in a truthful way. But historical, or collective, atonement has to be simultaneously worked out in individual relationships. Both of these processes begin and end in God's own atonement 'worked out' *with* and *for* us in the person of Jesus Christ.

Atonement and the Church

Losing sight of the solidarity which exists between God and human beings in the person of Jesus Christ leads to serious misunderstandings about the Christian faith, as well as the Church. For one thing, it has created the impression that Christianity is a religion which manipulates and damages the individual and that the Church is a hierarchical and largely male-dominated institution which exists to maintain the status quo by reinforcing feelings of personal guilt or inadequacy. This gives the impression that the Christian faith is manipulative and that the Church uses the Christian doctrines of atonement and redemption to exercise its power, although many Christians are only too aware of the Church's need for forgiveness for its own past, up to and including the present day.

> It has given rise to the idea that Christianity manipulates and damages the individual

> It has created the impression that the Church uses the Christian doctrines of atonement and redemption to exercise its power

For Christians, their relationship with God is being worked out in the dynamic presence of Christ, his Holy Spirit, working in and through his Church on earth, a Church of which they are an integral part.[5] When the institutional Church gets in the way of this work, through its divisions and conflicts and increasingly secular priorities, it sends out some very confusing messages about the unconditional love of God and the values and priorities of his kingdom. These messages undermine the Church's own faith in the reality of God's unconditional forgiveness and so help to perpetuate, in the minds of many people who do not go to church, a picture of a vindictive God whose only concern is to remind people of their shortcomings and general unworthiness. In other words, blocking forgiveness in its own life makes it difficult for the Church to be a channel of forgiveness to the secular world.

> **This makes it difficult for the Church to be a channel of forgiveness**

God, atonement and people

These ideas about the Church not only misrepresent God but also give a false idea of the nature of culpability, and here I would like to distinguish between culpability and guilt. Briefly stated, culpability involves taking responsibility for the effect of wrong actions, while guilt is the result of the imposition of that culpability through judgement or blame. With the free owning of responsibility comes forgiveness. With judgement come guilt and condemnation. Feelings of guilt reduce any sense of responsibility for the consequences of our words and actions to the fear of punishment. This has the effect of removing, or at least obscuring, the healthy regret which a person ought to feel when he or she has wronged someone else.[6]

Fear of punishment is ultimately ego-driven and feelings of guilt and denial will allow us to contrive any number of ways to avoid it. One of these allows a person to avoid responsibility for what has occurred, as well as for putting matters to right. Avoiding responsibility comes with adopting the position of victim, which is not the same as being presumed to be a soft target in the sense I described earlier. In this context, being a victim is a means of exercising control over others through guilt. In other words, it is always someone else's fault that things are the way they are and it is always with someone else that the blame lies. Governments are blamed and individuals often held unfairly to account for everything that is wrong in society, all of which conveniently ignores the fact that it is we who vote governments into power in the first place, so there is perhaps some truth in the saying that we get the governments we deserve.[7]

The victim mentality also allows those who may have been wronged, and are therefore genuine victims, to avoid taking responsibility for repairing the damage done to themselves or to a third party, including the perpetrator. Sadly, we see this syndrome occurring in the context of the most righteous causes. Minority groups allow themselves to continue to be seen as the victims of injustice, even when the injustice has begun to be put right. In some cases, a whole group continues to be blamed for their suffering, irrespective of the efforts and sacrifices made by many individuals to see justice done; as when all men are seen as sexist, or all women as power-hungry men-haters. All of this hostility is fuelled by fear. Fear now becomes the source of the two most pernicious effects of wrongdoing on the human person and on relationships between people in the wider contexts of history and society. These are the fear of retribution, from God as well as from people, and the fear of other people for other indirectly related reasons. By allowing these two closely related fears to subtly dominate their moral consciousness, human beings have wrought all manner of destruction upon themselves and upon the world.

Jesus Christ enters into this destruction and takes into himself the pain which it causes. In other words, he takes responsibility for it. In so doing, he inaugurates an entirely new and completely effective approach to the overcoming of fear by meeting human beings in their own fear and in the alienation which it causes. He himself becomes 'alienated'. He experiences what it means to be an outcast, to 'not belong' in the context of human relationships. At the same time, he remains profoundly connected to us in love. In the perfection of his own divine nature, he fully identifies with our fear of retribution by accepting the inevitable consequence of what is a very *human* desire for 'payback'. The Christian idea of atonement involves an ongoing 'working' relationship between a loving Creator and his people from within the scene of devastation itself and from within God's own being: in other words, from within the life of the Trinity.[8]

> **The Christian idea of atonement involves an ongoing 'working' relationship between God and people**

We get glimpses of the ongoing relational life of the Trinity, and the freedom of God's love, as it is reflected in the love which surfaces when human beings work together to rebuild and make good the evil and destruction of war.[9] We see it also in the courageous love of people caught up in major disasters as, for example, in the London Blitz of 1940, Sarajevo in the 1990s, New York in 2002 and Haiti in 2010. All of these are examples of the potential for a human response to God's invitation to be in relationship with him in his ongoing work of salvation in which love overcomes fear, and the desire to heal breaks down enmity.[10] The Christian understanding of atonement involves, first, a recognition of our need for healing and for the renewal of relationship, and second, overcoming the kind of fear which obliges us to protect ourselves from retributive punishment. So how is it that we have lost sight of the way God's atoning work, his being with and for us, heals and reconciles us to him and to one another?

Atonement and the Bible – the Old Testament legacy

In order to address these questions Christians need to re-evaluate where they are coming from in their own history as it relates to that of God's people, the Jews. One of the criticisms levelled at Christians is that they have appropriated the Scriptures which were first given to the Jews, in order to explain and justify the atoning work of Christ. The way in which Christians read Scripture as pointing to the salvation of the whole human race therefore becomes very problematic when the three Abrahamic religions, Christianity, Islam and Judaism, are seen to be fundamentally in conflict with each other and not the joint heirs of a single Abrahamic legacy. This is because, in relation to the atoning work of Christ, Scripture appears to speak of a once and for all event, a promise made to Abraham concerning a particular people. But Christ's reconciling work of atonement applies in equal measure to anyone who wants it, irrespective of ethnicity or gender. He suffers and dies not only as a Jew, but as the 'second Adam', the one who holds the whole human race in his own humanity.

God's reconciling work is also ongoing, a dynamic and living process of healing and of restoring human beings into relationship with God, as promised to Abraham, set down in the covenant and realized in Christ up to and including the present day. This dynamic movement is the ongoing working presence of the Holy Spirit in history, and history is to be read contextually if we are to learn from it today. Events are shaped by cultural circumstances, or contexts, and can only be fully understood within those contexts. They also take place at a particular point in time and for specific reasons. All of these considerations need to be taken into account when we think of the atonement as it is presented in Scripture.

The social or cultural contexts in which God's work of atonement is described in the Old Testament are already shaped by the culture of the indigenous people of Canaan, and later of Egypt and Babylon. In all three of these contexts the idea of a God who desires to be known and loved by his people would have been unimaginable. On the whole, these early civilizations would also have found it very difficult to conceive of a God who did not need to be appeased, or who could not be worshipped in the form of inanimate objects or through the spirit world. Early Canaanite and Babylonian worshippers explained God to themselves through stories and myths in order to try to make sense of what they believed to be the supreme life force at work in the world. They also domesticated their idea of God by making him 'tangible'. They erected 'shrines' and fashioned 'gods' from wood or stone to which they sacrificed animals and sometimes even children.

These sacrifices were designed to appease a wrathful deity and to persuade him to act in the interest of his worshippers by blessing their crops and protecting them from disease and aggression. Sacrifice was so closely bound to the cultic myth that it became part of it, both as a visual enactment of a people's own self-understanding in relation to these gods and as a visual re-enactment of the whole story of the created order and human existence. The story was simple and dualistic, a battle between the destructive forces of nature and the survival of humanity, between light and darkness and good and evil. In this kind of sacrificial thought-world human beings acted both as mediators between these opposing forces and as servants of the creator god, Baal or, in the case of Babylon, Marduk. Sacrifice was the principal language of worship.

Allowing for the fact that much of Genesis was written after the second exile, when monotheism was more firmly established, Abraham's obedience and faith introduced the idea of monotheism into a particular culture context and it is from this context that the relationship between sacrifice and atonement was originally forged. For the early Israelites, the atoning work of sacrifice emphasized a separation between a holy God and an impure people. This separating of the holy from the 'profane' had two long-lasting effects on the way Christians think about atonement. First, atonement and holiness became closely associated with the concept of purity, leading to a conceptualization of God as distant, jealous and vengeful. He was a God who was only concerned with retribution for sins, which were usually an infringement of laws relating to purity.[11] These laws were a means of setting the people of God apart from the surrounding nations, endowing them with a clear identity, and of maintaining a sense of the holy and the sacred in relation to God himself.[12]

Second, these portrayals of an essentially violent God encourage us to think of Christ's atonement as a violent event. Allowing Christian theology to be coloured by a violent perception of God can make Christians violent towards others, and ultimately leads to triumphalist attitudes towards other Christians, or towards other faiths. Between Christians, this violent attitude stems from a fundamental distrust of those who do not understand Christian atonement as primarily concerned with God's retributive and violent punishment for sin, and as taking precedence over God's reciprocal loving relationship with his people. In the Old Testament, God journeys (literally 'tents') with his people as a sign of his covenant with them, that he is in solidarity with his people, so that over time they might learn to shape their priorities on the basis of being in right relationship with him, on a desire to know and be known by God. For Christians, this desire is met and consummated in the atoning work of Jesus Christ.

> **These encourage us to think of Christ's atonement as a violent event**

Atonement and the Bible – the New Testament

The New Testament embodies the fulfilment of God's promise and is also known as the New Covenant. The relationship which until now has been reserved for God's own people, the Jews, now embraces all of humanity. It is brought about by the transformation of the human predicament from one of alienation from God to one of reconciliation and friendship. The covenant embrace we experience in Jesus can be compared to two long-standing friends who have been separated by a quarrel and are now reunited. The healing and reconciliation which takes place between them is of such depth that it is as if they are seeing each other both for the first time and as if they had never been apart. The relationship between human beings and God, as a result of God's atoning work in Christ, brings a new intimacy between him and those who accept his invitation to be 'at one' with him.

Throughout his life, the friendships and healing encounters which Jesus has with people from every kind of background are intimate, as if he has always known the person in question. He knows about the past life of the Samaritan woman who says of him, '[He] told me everything I have ever done',[13] not because he is a clairvoyant, but because he knows her as a uniquely created and loved child of God. In his encounter with the woman brought to him by the religious authorities who were about to stone her for adultery, he knows their own perfidious nature and literally spells it out to them in the sand.[14] He also knows the full set of circumstances which have brought the woman to this point in her life. In this respect, it is perhaps worth noting that while he tells her to 'go your way, and from now on do not sin again', it is not immediately obvious that the sin consists only in adultery. In terms of the Jewish law it almost certainly did, but in terms of the values which Jesus had come to inaugurate, and which define the kingdom of God, it may well have been the *consequence* of her adultery which most concerned him. She may have caused great pain to others, as well as to herself, in neglecting or abusing people close to her. It is these underlying consequences which have to do with the well-being of human beings that concern Jesus as much, if not more, than the law itself.

Jesus comes therefore to inaugurate a new era, a kingdom in which outworn values and priorities which distance God from his people and reinforce the authority of a powerful religious elite are now reversed. His conversation with Nicodemus, himself a Pharisee, revolves around the subject of rebirth and the dynamic life of the Holy Spirit working in a person who knows God from the heart, as well as with the mind.[15] Jesus picks up on Nicodemus' lack of spiritual insight. Despite the fact that he is an expert in Jewish law, Nicodemus is only able to see God through the prism of this law. He is a rational thinker, who has not yet experienced the kind of need for God which would give meaning and substance to his theology.

Unlike Nicodemus, the woman who was healed of an incurable haemorrhage 'knew' that if she only touched Jesus' garment she would be healed. Her intuitive 'knowing' was the knowledge of faith which allowed her to draw close to Jesus and enabled his healing to take effect.[16] The blind man who interrupted Jesus as he was teaching, with loud cries to the Son of David for mercy, was making a similar 'movement of faith'.[17] Both of these incidents, and others like them, depict a covenant movement, a movement which makes two people 'at one' with each other and, as in the case of the people Jesus healed, at one with their own bodies and with God. Taken together, they suggest that the Christian idea of atonement begins in a deeper understanding of the significance of the life of Jesus, as well as of his death. The cross is the consummation of his life and of God's promise to be 'at one' with all who recognize their need for God and turn to him in a relationship with his Son.

Atonement in Jesus Christ

The Christian idea of atonement in Jesus Christ is revolutionary. It turns the things we take for granted about forgiveness and reparation, and the subsequent rebuilding of relationships, completely upside down. It does so by declaring that where there has been a wrong committed, things are set right without the wrongdoers having to be punished for what they have done or make reparation through some form of retributive moral 'pay-back' process. All that is required is a person's acceptance of his or her need for forgiveness and of God's grace.

Why then was it necessary for Christ to actually die for our sins? Many people are understandably put off Christianity by the idea that the brutal sacrifice of God's own Son was necessary in order to make us worthy of salvation. Even before they try to come to terms with the need for this sacrifice, they instinctively recoil from a God who seems to require it. In fact, everything I have said so far about God's reconciling work, as well as the healing and forgiveness which embodies atonement, makes no sense at all in the context of such a requirement. But just as the kingdom which Jesus inaugurates during his earthly life reverses all the priorities of the old law, the sacrifice of his death is also of a different order. In order to make sense of it, we need to remember that this sacrifice had nothing in common with the sacrificial methods of the past in which animals were slaughtered as a way of 'paying for' sin and assuaging an angry deity.

The sacrifice of Christ begins from the moment of his conception, in God's decision to be wholly involved with the human predicament. Paul, using a hymn adapted from a non-Judaic source, describes this engagement with humanity as 'God . . . being born in human likeness. And being found in human form, he humbled himself and became obedient to the point of death – even death on a cross.'[18] It is with his acceptance of death itself that the key to making sense of atonement lies. The death of Christ was not simply imposed by the Father. Jesus could have refused it, and was tempted to do so in the Garden of Gethsemane where he prayed on the night he was arrested. Neither was it the case that death alone was necessary to set to rights the relationship between God and humanity. The sacrifice of Christ is that of a whole life lived to God and an acceptance of suffering and of human mortality as part of that life and part of the *consequence* of human sin. But even the acceptance of death would not alone have proved that human beings are ultimately destined for eternal life with God.

The Christian idea of atonement only begins to make sense when the death of Christ is seen in the context of his life and resurrection. Christ's resurrection is sometimes treated as a kind of postscript to his Passion rather than as its central meaning and purpose. Christ entered fully into our human predicament and by his dying and rising redeemed the human race from alienation and ultimate oblivion. In the final chapter of this book I shall have more to say on how the resurrection of Christ is the ultimate sign of redemption for the human race, but for the moment it is enough to say that Christ experiences *with* us and *for* us the depths of desolation, of God-forsakenness, on the cross.

This brings us a little closer to understanding in what sense his suffering and dying was a 'punishment' for sin. The 'punishment' was in fact God's Son deliberately taking into himself the inevitable *consequence* of humanity's tendency to give up on God, a tendency which results in its own self-destruction and in the destruction of God's world. Destruction is our

God's Son took into himself the *consequence* of humanity's tendency to give up on God

default position, insofar as we have a proclivity for protecting our selves and our perceived self-interests over those of others. God's loving of the world required that Christ reverse this trend in his birth, in all his relationships and in his dying. But why should this be necessary?

Conclusion

We begin to find an answer to this in contemplating the loneliness of human suffering. Christ owns this loneliness for himself. He also takes responsibility for the alienation human beings experience as a direct consequence of selfish living. The selfish act, from which all other destructive actions flow, is done to protect my own interests, to use others in order for me to feel safe and needed, but it has the reverse effect. The selfish person is ultimately the loneliest. In Christ's suffering we see him experiencing the very depths of this loneliness. This is his suffering 'with' humanity, rather than 'instead of' humanity. If Christ's act of obedience on the cross is reduced simply to an 'instead of' act, or what we call *propitiatory* atonement or *penal substitution*, we see only a very small and distorted part of the bigger picture. Christ dies *for* our sins because he chooses, with the whole of his life, to be *with* us in them by taking human sin into himself, as well as by accepting the consequences of sin. In this way, God in Christ dies from within his own self in order to meet people in their true selves.[19] He becomes as we are in order that we may become as he is.[20] When this happens, his divine nature is so joined with our human nature, without in any way being compromised or diminished by it, that our humanity is embraced by God and becomes a part of him. This raises a very important question. If we are changed by being so closely bound to God himself, how do we account for our ongoing complicity in the evil we see around us?

2

The problem of sin

What is sin? Are human beings inherently bad? Why does God allow evil? Why do good people suffer? Is there a difference between sin and evil? How important is motive in the choices we make?

What I have said in the last chapter suggests that human beings have always experienced a need for forgiveness and for belonging together. Historically, we could say that the transition from primate to human involved a gradual process of acquiring a sense of identity in community, of knowing who we are as individuals in relation to others and of learning to take responsibility for the way we communicate and relate to them. Humanity became *homo sapiens* from the moment people developed a more refined sense of relatedness, one which would ensure the survival of the community. They also sensed that they stood in some kind of dependent relatedness to a higher power, a power which they invested in the natural world but which also had to be bribed and placated through sacrifice.

Scripture describes how, with the arrival of monotheism, came the law of Moses, and a more precise understanding of wrongdoing and of how wrongdoing, or sin, affects human beings in relation to God and their relationships with one another. Paul says that 'through the law comes the knowledge of sin'.[1] In other words, it is impossible for human beings to be perfectly obedient to God's law, since human nature is naturally inclined to think and act in its own interests. These centre around what Paul calls the 'flesh', which is what we would call materialism and anything which diverts our affections from God to our own selfish and often short-term interests. Despite the law given by God to Moses, sin not only continued to damage human relationships but brought with it a complex set of problems regarding human nature itself. Were human beings naturally bad? If not, why were they unable to prevent this continual 'falling away' from God's law? The Bible opens with a story which attempts to make sense of these questions and to explain the nature of alienation, which is the price we pay for sin.

'Original' sin

Until fairly recently, and for some Christians today, the story at the beginning of Genesis has been read both as an actual event and as a morality tale, an example of what happens when human beings disobey God. On the basis of such a reading, when Adam and Eve took the forbidden apple they sinned against God and deserved to be punished. For us, the important significance of this allegory for sin is that it is essentially about covetousness. Adam and Eve disobeyed God's will for their greatest happiness and well-being in desiring to possess what God had forbidden in their own best interests and because it was his to forbid. Furthermore, the tendency to covet was passed on like an ineradicable family trait from one generation to the next, with the result that human beings were seen to have a propensity for wrongdoing which is essentially selfish. Human nature is therefore sinful and, if we follow this line of thinking to its logical conclusion, inherently bad.

Thomas Aquinas (1225–74) developed an understanding of sin as the logical consequence of wrong choices. Sin was a wilful decision to go against what was 'natural', in other words what had been ordained by God, for whom the well-being and happiness of human beings was an inherent part of his will. Aquinas' thinking also derived from the thought world of the Greeks, and of Aristotle in particular, for whom morality, or virtue, was neutral in regard to relationships. An action was virtuous to the extent that it brought about a morally good result. Moral values were both universal and self-evident. They did not have any particular bearing on relationships, for either better or worse. This led to Aquinas developing a theological ethic whereby the universality of a virtue, or value, became an end in itself and any action, even a violent one, was justified if the end was morally desirable. The ends justify the means in the way 'sparing the rod' was for a long time thought to 'spoil the child'.

If virtue is an objective or neutral value, and if the end always justifies the means, it has important implications for how we think about sin in relation to God. In many places, the Bible depicts a God who, in his meting out of punishment for wrong choices and sinful acts, appears both cruel and arbitrary in his judgements. Deportations, plagues, blights and natural disasters of cataclysmic proportions are punishments which seem out of all proportion to the wrong action. Allowing for the fact that the moral landscape in early biblical times was rugged in the extreme, these events portray a God who, in his use of force and violence, appears to be subject to two very human emotions, anger and vindictiveness.

On the other hand, the Adam and Eve story is the first of many Bible stories which also portray a God who grieves over the long-term effect of human sin on his relationship with the people he loves. The metaphorical exile from the garden is not simply God's sundering of their relationship, but the inevitability of cause and effect. Wrong choices lead to alienation. As far as God is concerned, the man and the woman are never unlovable but, as self-preoccupied individuals who have decided that they no longer trust or need God enough to warrant their staying within the limits he sets for them, they become estranged (literally, as strangers) from him. The story therefore shows sin to be the assertion of the autonomous individual's right to be free of God and of the constraints of his law, and the desire to be free of responsibility towards others.

We can also think of original sin as the consequence of becoming *homo sapiens*. As a conscious being, man (I use the term in its generic sense) is free to make choices. These choices will either strengthen community and family bonds, or weaken and even sever them. They are a way of speaking of the natural instinct for survival in moral terms, what Richard Dawkins calls the 'selfish gene'.[2] The instinct for survival was in itself morally neutral until the arrival of consciousness, or what we also call 'conscience'. Acting in accordance with the dictates of conscience, in relation to personal survival, is more complicated for a human being than it is for an animal. Animals are not moral creatures. They are neither selfish nor unselfish. They act on the basis of instinct, so that individual existence and the survival of the species become the equivalent of their moral framework, but their 'choices' are not moral ones.

Thinking of the Adam and Eve story in the context of human evolution helps us conceptualize it as a gradual transition from moral neutrality to moral consciousness.[3] For us, moral decisions are bound up with our relatedness to one another at the deeper level which we call love, a love which proceeds from a God who already loves us and informs our moral decision-making through the activity of God's free gift of grace. But the gift has to be willingly accepted. The Adam and Eve story is a metaphor showing what happens when human beings refuse God's grace in the mistaken belief that they can manage without it. This refusal of grace allows feelings of both guilt and shame to spoil their lives and disfigure the selves they were meant to become because, in asserting their independence from God, Adam and Eve acquire the knowledge of good and evil too soon. They lose their innocence in being literally 'seduced' by the unknown and the forbidden. This is humanity's first experience of betrayal. Metaphorically, they were duped by the enemy who assured them that in taking what was God's they would become 'like God'.[4] Instead, they are left with a profound sense of shame, a shame which makes them literally 'embarrassed' to be seen by him. Their embarrassment drives them into exile,[5] into the kind of alienation and chronic loneliness which I described in the last chapter.

Shame and guilt

Sin therefore has two very detrimental effects on the way we relate to God and to one another, because it brings with it shame about ourselves and guilt and regret about wrong actions. Earlier, I suggested that guilt is directly connected to conscious actions or thoughts and that these actions bring judgement, or blame. Shame is the result of alienation and brings with it intensely negative emotions with regard to our own self-worth.[6] Shame does not automatically imply guilt. In fact, it is felt all the more keenly when a person is not guilty. Nathanial Hawthorne, in *The Scarlet Letter*, explores the nature of shame in the context of innocence when a mother is exposed to public reprobation with her young daughter for an act for which she was not responsible. She had been raped by the pastor of the town. Irrespective of whether a person is the victim or the perpetrator, the memory of a wrong action is bound up with that person's sense of self. It is through this sense of shame, and the way it spoils the true self, that Augustine, writing in the latter part of the third century, arrived at his own understanding of sin.

In his *Confessions* Augustine realizes that he has confused ambition, intellect and human desire with his need for God, a theme which informs the whole of his work. The earlier part of the book deals with a sense of shame concerning his past. His journey to faith is a return from exile, similar to the exile of Adam and Eve. But where Adam and Eve begin in a state of innocence and only later acquire the consciousness of good and evil, Augustine looks back on his childhood and youth as a time of wilful ignorance. He believes that this state of wilful ignorance, or estrangement from God, is bequeathed to all human beings from their first parents, in the moment that Adam and Eve made a conscious choice to disobey God. The main problem with Augustine's thinking lies in his identifying *original* sin with procreation and in his interpretation of the Adam and Eve story as an actual historical event. Not only does the story fail to conform to historical and archaeological research, but when viewed in this way it makes guilt and shame something all human beings must accept as an unavoidable part of the human condition which they inherit from their first parents in the act of procreation itself.

This in turn leads to a view that human beings are inherently sinful, or bad, and has had a negative influence on Christian doctrine over the centuries, especially with regard to the meaning and purpose of baptism. Instead of being a sign of welcome and acceptance into God's family, baptism becomes a literal 'washing away' of original sin, implying that there is some innate defect in God's creation. It also suggests that God must have had a direct involvement in creating sin itself, rather than sinful actions being entirely down to the conscious choice of a mature human being.

Augustine's thinking on the inherent sinfulness of human beings also derived from his earlier life when he was closely associated with the followers of Mani. The Manichees, as they were called, believed that the physical world and especially the human body and procreation were essentially bad, or contaminated. The elite among them dedicated themselves to a life of sexual abstinence and asceticism and the sect had a profound influence on the way Augustine thought about sin. Although his thinking resembles that of Thomas Aquinas, particularly with regard to wrong choices, these wrong choices affect Augustine at a much deeper level. Subjective feelings combine with an objective knowledge of his intellectual abilities and rhetorical gifts which, until his conversion, he feels he has used for his own advancement or satisfaction rather than in the service of God. As a result of these conflicting emotions, Augustine is burdened with a sense of guilt. But at the same time, he is able to discern the activity of grace which has obliged him to come to terms with his need for God. He realizes that despite his intellectual talent and personal gifts he is spiritually destitute. In the light of modern psychology, we might be tempted to say that this 'poverty' of spirit is the neurotic self-obsession of a troubled individual attempting to make sense of who he is in the light of his past. But this is to misunderstand Augustine and the nature of his confessions. Their real significance lies in reminding the reader of a particular and universal need for God which human beings must acknowledge if they are to be at peace with themselves and with others. Augustine describes this need as a God-shaped 'space' in the most secret part of the human self. In his *Confessions* he writes '. . . you have made us for yourself, and our heart is restless until it

Sin is therefore a matter of denying God to oneself

rests in you'.[7] Sin is therefore not simply a matter of committing certain acts, or of indulging in destructive thoughts, but of denying God to oneself.

Sin and evil

The Adam and Eve metaphor for sin involves a unilateral claim for autonomous freedom for human beings. But the price paid for this freedom is a sundering of all their relationships, and not only the particular bond of trust and love which they had with God. Metaphorically speaking, Adam and Eve's sin has brought about a profound breakdown in trust between humanity and the rest of creation. The Tower of Babel story is a kind of re-enactment of Eden itself.[8] It is a story about breakdown in human relationships on a social level, as well as a metaphor for the disruption of harmony in creative work. The communication breakdown on the tower is not only about the loss of a common language. It also suggests a more profound rupture of the kind of empathy which enables good social partnerships, the ability to intuit what others are about or what makes them who they are. In the Babel story, the breakdown in verbal communication means that human beings no longer have the empathy needed to carry on God's creative work within the limits set for them, both individually and as a community. They can no longer connect with one another. Like Adam and Eve, the builders of the tower have infringed certain boundaries, the limits to understanding and knowledge set by God for that particular time, but that does not mean that God is against the pursuit of knowledge or of scientific inquiry as such.

In the Babel story, as in the context of Eden, rebellion and impatience are revealed as two aspects of the same sin within the evolutionary process of our becoming 'conscious' beings, but this time moral awareness concerns relationship, not only with God but with other human beings. In both of these contexts there are essential choices to be made. Right choices ought logically to lead to good outcomes, but human suffering seems to contradict this. Since 'goodness' is not entirely down to human choice and does not invariably lead to a good outcome, we must assume that, metaphorically speaking, evil is at work to prevent this happening. But speaking of evil as an objective entity which is 'at work' can lead to further misinterpretations of the Garden of Eden story, most notably that knowledge is itself evil and that the quest for knowledge, including scientific enquiry, somehow puts God to the test. This is to ignore a crucial factor concerning knowledge. Knowledge is resourced in what the Bible calls Wisdom, which is an aspect of God himself. It follows that the pursuit of all knowledge is the pursuit of God, a desire to enter more deeply into what Paul calls 'the mind of God' and thereby to arrive at a deeper relationship with him and a better understanding of his loving purpose for the whole of creation.

The pursuit of knowledge is only perverted when it is driven by the desire for power. In his book, *The Future of Man*, Pierre Teilhard de Chardin describes a moment of realization, or consciousness, that a certain kind of scientific knowledge will bring with it the power to harness and control energy in a way that will have lethal consequences on a vast scale. This is not because the knowledge in question is inherently evil, but because the desire for power which can motivate the quest for knowledge is corrupting when power-driven motives are not held in check by a higher sense of responsibility for the consequences of certain actions.[9]

In many of his letters, Paul describes his own struggles to overcome temptation as a motivational dilemma. He sees the motives which inform his actions as intrinsic to a conflict with evil, a battle between 'flesh and spirit', taking place within his own consciousness.[10] In speaking of evil as something real, rather than as an abstract philosophical concept, Paul was also able to make sense of the difference between sin as wrong choice and sin as something unavoidable, brought about by the prohibitions of the Jewish law. But this does not entirely explain the problem of evil. If sin is a matter of lawbreaking or of wrong choices leading to wrong actions, evil would appear to be the force which compels human beings to act sinfully, and not simply a dark entity proceeding from some other realm. Evil is at work within the heart of the individual and within the infrastructures of society.

This brings evil a little closer to home and obliges human beings to take responsibility for the evil which they allow. It calls for an engagement with the way evil goes on evolving and working within history on a social as well as on an individual scale. To ignore evil is to practise a form of quietism, a passive non-engagement with the testing questions of faith, especially where those questions need to be addressed within the context of politics and social responsibility. Dietrich Bonhoeffer, in his resistance to the official Nazi Church, deplored the kind of passivity which allowed many Christians to ignore the evil of Hitler's propaganda and the way in which it was infiltrating the Church. Bonhoeffer was to found the Confessing Church which resisted this evil from within and, like martyrs before and after him, it was resistance to social and political evil which cost

Bonhoeffer his life. Taking responsibility for evil requires awareness and a willingness to engage personally and, if practical, proactively with the evils of society. The end of evil regimes and social systems has come about because people have been willing to get personally involved through protest and active resistance.

There is also a spiritual dimension to evil which calls for a different kind of resistance, the resistance of intercessory prayer. The extent to which prayer is or is not efficacious is, of course, unquantifiable. We will never know how many millions of people were praying for an end to the South African apartheid regime and we can never prove what difference it would have made had they not been praying. Nevertheless, as Christians, we are called to resist evil by standing against it from within ourselves.

Prayerful resistance to evil involves a kind of two-way mindfulness in which a person is fully present to God and at the same time fully and compassionately present to evil and to the suffering it causes. This is what Jesus describes as worship which flows like living water from the centre of human consciousness and of human self-understanding.[11] Worship connects us to God and in so doing allows us to confront evil as a definable enemy and as a spiritual 'dis-ease' in our relationship with God.[12] But if evil is to be confronted by engaging more deeply with God, this begs the question of why God allows evil to happen in the first place and why it is that those who least deserve it seem to be the victims of the greatest misfortune.

Job's questioning of God

The book of Job is an allegorical portrayal of one man's attempt to make sense of how God seems to afflict those who least deserve it. Job's book is about the nature of faith. It is a conversation between Job and his so-called friends, who wrongly accuse him and try to persuade him that he deserves his misfortunes. It is also about Job's vital relationship with a living God. What is important about the book is that it reveals how faith allows for questions and active protest rather

> **It reveals how faith allows for questions and active protest**

than passive acquiescence to a set of beliefs which no longer connect with our own experience of suffering. In his dialogue with the three 'comforters' who are sent by God to assist Satan[13] in the testing of his servant, Job takes responsibility for himself in his predicament, rather than blaming someone else for what has happened to him. This 'owning' of his situation is neither passive acceptance nor an admission of guilt. He actively questions God and this has the potential for getting God to 'change his mind', which God does on a number of occasions in Scripture.[14] Job is a virtuous man who can prove that he has led a blameless life, so if this is simply an endurance test set by God to prove Job's resilience to temptation, what does it say about Satan and about God himself?

Satan is a complex figure. He has not always been seen as the personification of evil, but as the agent of testing. Satan is also described as Lucifer, the angel of light and, in the context of the creation myth, God's most trusted servant. But he is also a figurative representation of what happens when lust for power turns to envy. He becomes a destructive force at work against God's good and loving purpose. We might also think of Satan as the evil or destructive tendency operating within the structures and systems in which we find ourselves and within which we make choices which affect our own lives as well as the lives of some of the poorest and most vulnerable.

In his dialogue with the 'accusers' who work alongside Satan, Job is defending a way of life which seems to indicate that, given the particular circumstances of his position and of the times in which he lived, he made the right choices for the right reasons. This has important implications for the way we think about sin and choice and the extent to which the individual is able to take responsibility for sinful structures and systems. Although Job is not a historical figure, since the story is not a historical account of actual events, we can assume that, as a person of means, his wealth derived from the particular social structure of his times. At the beginning of the story God asks Satan if, in his wandering across the earth, he has met anyone as righteous as his servant Job, one who knew how to prosper with integrity in an essentially fallen world perhaps comparable to our own, a world made up of legal systems and structures which were morally flawed.

Righteousness in today's world

Like Job, we do not simply give up on making moral decisions within the structures that govern modern life, but seek to understand how we might work with God in and through the choices we make. This influences the way we think about God in the context of sin and of a human condition which is marked by suffering, most often of those who least deserve it. The victims of climate change and world conflicts are invariably the poorest and the most vulnerable. Job shows us that engaging with God from within this fallen condition involves being prepared to yield our rational understanding into the love of God without either turning our back on reality or refusing to engage intelligently with the difficult questions of faith. It is because of his initial failure to understand the depth and scope of God's love, and God's power to transcend suffering, that Job repents 'in dust and ashes'. He is not repenting of having had the temerity to argue with God, or to protest against unjust suffering. Instead, the book affirms that God has involved himself in the consequences of evil, and that it is only in this sense that he allows suffering. Furthermore, Job's experience reveals that it is often as victims of evil and in the context of suffering that people experience God most closely. Experiencing God in the context of suffering and adversity, and in the context of modern life, may seem beyond most of us because we are overwhelmed by too many pressing concerns for this to be possible.

Sown among thistles

In his parable about the sower, Jesus compares the person whose life is full of distractions that overwhelm his or her sense of God to seed which has been sown among thistles.[15] While a seed cannot be blamed for having been sown in the wrong place, the story illustrates the way distractions from God surround and consume human beings in the particular contextualities which shape their lives. For the relatively affluent, it is easy to see how the pressures of maintaining a lifestyle can very quickly supplant any sense of the meaning and purpose of life itself, especially in regard to relationships. Having to compromise between career and relationship can also bring feelings of guilt and shame because of the tendency to make comparisons with how things were done in the past. But the social contextuality in which lifestyle choices were made fifty years ago was entirely different from that of today. Making moral judgements about the way people lead their lives on the basis of what was taken for granted in previous generations only produces more guilt and resentment. On the other hand, a life of absolute detachment from 'the world' is available only to the very few and comes, in any case, with its own set of temptations. What *is* available, however, is the exciting possibility of experiencing God's love in the moment of turning to him from within the rush and uncertainty of daily life now.

If this is so, the parable of the sower needs to be read anew, especially in regard to the seed which fell among thistles. Seeing this story in the context of life as it is today, in the mainly affluent West, helps us refine our understanding of sin. Sin is not simply a matter of allowing worldly concerns to distract us from God, but of the real motive for any one choice. Discerning the truth about what motivates choice can be further complicated by the guilt associated with the actual enjoyment of that choice. A mother with a career, for example, may work for the sake of her own happiness, from which her children benefit, as well as for financial reasons, but in terms of the guilt she might experience she pays a double price for doing so. She feels a sense of real loss, not only at leaving a young child in someone else's care, especially if the child is unwell or unhappy, but also because she leaves home feeling relieved at the prospect of having a few hours' life-space in the context of her career. To suppress this happiness would be dishonest. It would also deny God the freedom to work to the good within the choices she makes, provided she loves him and tries to live in a way which is consistent with his purpose for the good of those who depend on her.[16] Furthermore, the mother in question is not an entirely autonomous agent. Whatever her motives, her choices are conditioned by a system which is itself inherently flawed. The system is the context which both defines the morality and conditions the decisions she makes. In other words, the rightness or wrongness of an attitude or action can change according to the expectations generated within the social or political mores of the time.[17]

Systemic evil

These mores are shaped or influenced by a number of changes and developments, including those of science and medical research. Take, for example, the change in the public's attitude to smoking which, as a result of medical research, has moved from indifference, to tolerance, to regarding it as a socially unacceptable practice bordering on sin. Furthermore, before cigarette advertisements were banned, smokers were simply the consumers of cigarettes, rather than people whose lives were being put at risk. I use this example not to pass judgement on smokers but to illustrate the way in which a commercially profitable enterprise can carry on operating without taking responsibility for the damage it causes to human lives.

> This leads to systems which are exploitative and thereby inherently evil

The same will soon be true in relation to instant or fast food companies and outlets. Failure to take responsibility for consumer choices leads to commercial and political systems, the two often being interrelated, which are exploitative and thereby inherently evil.

An even more disturbing example of systemic evil is the questionable morality of the so-called free market economy itself. This is far from being an even playing field. It is probably fair to say that what keeps the ball rolling is the inherent selectivity of success, beginning with the kind of start a person has in life. Success, in the form of an education paid for by even relatively successful parents, puts a person in a position to engage with a highly competitive world. At the same time, as Stephen Green describes in his book *Good Value*, there has been a significant change in what he calls the 'geopolitical reality' with regard to productivity and wealth.[18] The shift of economic weight from former colonial powers and from the United States to India, China and parts of the Middle East makes it difficult for the West to call upon those countries to exercise restraint in their impact on the environment and to observe basic employment rights. Given our own history and the extent to which we have exploited and damaged the world and its people, we in the West are not in a position to issue any kind of ultimatum in these areas to other countries.

Conclusion

So far, I have focused on the problem of sin and the extent to which sin mars our relationship with God and with one another. Our relationship with God, or lack of it, not only affects the way we deal with systemic evil, but is bound up with the way we think about ourselves as being in any sense 'worthy' or deserving of love and the extent to which we are accountable for the well-being of others. Both of these areas pertain to sin and consequently to shame, guilt and alienation. In order to begin to make sense of the Christian doctrine of atonement, we now need to examine some of the consequences of sin and alienation from God's own perspective in the context of the suffering of his Son.

3

The 'wrath' of God

Is God really good? Or just? Does he only love good people?
How can death on a cross be about life? In what sense is it
a victory? Why do we need forgiveness from God? How does
God forgive? How do we forgive those who don't ask for
forgiveness – or deserve it?

The Garden of Eden story is a helpful allegory for showing how sin
and evil destroy human beings from within, by persuading them that
they do not need God and, at the same time, that they are unworthy
of love and do not in some sense 'belong' with others. It illustrates
the effect of sin in terms of shame and alienation. Paradoxically,
sin also feeds on the illusion of self-righteousness and on the desire
for power and recognition which often accompanies it. The desire
for power causes us to mistake death for life in the pursuit of the
material, or what Paul calls 'the flesh', whether this is money, status
or success. Material things and aspirations, when they become the
primary motivator of a person's life, lead that person away from
God, who is the source of life itself,[1] and further into what we might
call evil.

The evil which gives rise to sin is a kind of nihilism, the bland-
ness and boredom which can take over people's lives, along with the
sense that nothing really matters. Terry Eagleton, in his book *On
Evil*,[2] describes evil as, among other things, fundamentally against all
that is created. Evil is cynicism, a complete denial of the good or of
the possibility for good in people. Cynicism takes over the human
psyche and blurs our moral vision. It deadens and destroys human
creativity and the good of which human beings are capable when
they are in a healthy relationship with God. Augustine speaks of
this relationship as a corollary of good itself, so that the deeper the
relationship with God, the greater the good.[3] Being receptive to God,

or refusing him, ultimately governs how human beings live their lives and the extent to which a person becomes an instrument of life or of death. Sin therefore includes every action, remark or gesture, whether of colleague, friend or parent, and every political decision, whether of state, organization or Church, which deadens and defeats human creativity and the potential for life.

Is God good?

Paul describes sin as deriving from his 'unspiritual' nature. It makes him 'a slave to the law of sin' which brings death.[4] Paul is speaking of a spiritual death, which for today's readers involves the gradual diminishment of the human person through some kind of destructive lifestyle, often involving maladaptive coping practices which try to deal with internalized guilt and shame.[5] These feelings, and the way they are dealt with, can also reflect a distorted view of God. For those whose self-worth has been diminished through the way God has been presented to them, God can seem both vindictive and violent, with the result that many such people ultimately give up on Christianity altogether. Fear of God does not mean that we should be frightened of him, but that we should allow ourselves to be drawn more deeply into his own life. This is what it means to be happy in the fullest sense. Happiness is the immediate and unconditional experience of God's grace, goodness and holiness in the ordinary and everyday.

Seeing God as angry and vindictive generates the wrong kind of fear of God and creates a corresponding distortion of the idea of his goodness.[6] If God needs to be bribed and appeased in order to make us worthy of happiness, happiness becomes his side of a bargain delivered only with great reluctance. This not only makes him appear stingy and malicious but also turns human goodness into a commodity, a kind of currency with which to buy God's favour. When Paul speaks of the 'fruits of the Spirit' he is not only speaking of virtues, but of the transformation of the human person from a state of alienation to one of graced goodness.[7] The

> **Happiness becomes his side of a bargain delivered only with great reluctance**

fruits of the spirit are the fruits of God's love at work in a person's life enabling that person to freely give the love he or she has freely received. Where goodness, or virtue, is simply the means with which to buy God's favour, virtue becomes detached from love. In other words, commodifying goodness reinforces the idea of virtue as something to be achieved through one's own efforts, with God being the ultimate judge of whether or not we deserve to be rewarded. This is psychologically damaging and creates real obstructions in a person's faith journey. It also distorts one of the key Christian virtues, that of humility.

Over the centuries, the Church has allowed humility to be reduced to a matter of submission and obedience, too often at the expense of women's sense of self-worth and purpose.[8] This partial understanding of humility, a word derived from the Latin *humus*, meaning soil and implying gestation and growth, is life-destroying rather than life-giving. The Rule of Saint Benedict, who was the founder of Western monasticism, teaches a far more creative and life-nurturing humility, one which is grounded in love between the brethren and in the abbot's love and care for those in his charge. It reflects the humility taught by Christ which he embraced in his living and dying. Christ's humility was entirely shaped by love. He became as human beings are in order to draw close to them, first as a child in the context of trusting relationships with his earthly family and later in accepting betrayal at the hands of his friends and a death which was caused by human envy.

At the time of Christ's teaching ministry, the law served as a reminder to God's people of his holiness, his awesomeness. The Covenant enshrined a promise to them of God's faithfulness while at the same time reinforcing a sense of distance between God and his people. God's holiness made him both untouchable and unknowable, and priests who served in the inner sanctuary of the Temple were required to be in a state of ritual purity.[9] God's covenant promise to his people and his holiness and ineffability combine to give a picture of a God who is loving and faithful to his promises, but at the same time distant. He journeys with his people and leads them out of exile, but is hidden in a cloud by day and in fire by night, evoking both the mystery of God and the depth and intensity of his involvement with humanity. His commandments are conditional, but clear. He honours his promises but brings his wrath to bear on those who transgress his laws. Although this portrayal of God goes some way towards mitigating the severe picture of him given in other parts of the Old Testament, we are still left with a very one-sided understanding of the atoning work of God in the cross of Christ. How could a merciful and just God who so identifies with his people still oblige his own Son to be killed in order to atone for their sins?

The death of Christ and the wrath of God

Such a view suggests that God is not only vindictive and cruel but a most unnatural parent. What father would want to see his son tortured, publicly shamed and executed for the sake of winning back a people who are completely indifferent to him? If this concept of God and of his dealing with sin is the only way to think about the atonement, it is hardly surprising that it has left such a legacy of guilt and shame. Thinking of atonement exclusively in these terms has had the opposite effect on many people's attitude to God from that which he intended. Instead of reaching a deeper and more trusting relationship with him in the kind of mature self-awareness which leads to genuine repentance, they find themselves unable to be rid of feelings of guilt and of the deep shame they associate with the punishment meted out to Jesus for their sins.

> **Thinking of atonement exclusively in these terms has had the opposite effect on many people's attitude to God**

When I was engaged in pastoral ministry, I sometimes asked people to write down the feelings they experienced as a result of having dwelt exclusively on this substitutionary theory of atonement. One such person wrote about her feelings of guilt in relation to the cross as follows:

This is something I've come across frequently – that I personally crucified Jesus . . . Even though I wasn't there, nor there during the fall in the Garden of Eden, I am still personally responsible for this appalling death . . . The cross has been coupled for me with deep self-loathing and condemnation – it is almost as if I am that bad, that vile and wretched that my very being and character demanded a price of ruthless proportions.

Groups and powerful individuals exacerbate these negative feelings when they control or abuse the people they are meant to serve.[10] When people are manipulated by someone else, be it a church leader or a close friend or partner, they have nowhere to place their guilty feelings. Their anger becomes internalized and this 'blocks' their progress towards a truthful relationship with God, one which ought to be forged out of questioning and protest, and grounded in trust. The person quoted above also speaks, in relation to a doctrine of purely substitutionary atonement, of the moral confusion which surrounds the question of anger itself:

> I struggle with the idea of the fundamental wrongness of certain emotions – in particular anger – and the correlating command to 'overcome' this emotion, rather than truly confess it . . . and allow it to be channelled with all its energy into good. So often it seems those teaching this perspective ignore some of the gut-wrenching cries of the psalms, and the passionate anger of God. It would be wonderful if we could embrace this more as Christians.

These feelings are not uncommon, so that if we are to make any sense of the atoning work of God in Jesus Christ we need to broaden our understanding of the word 'wrath' which makes God's anger seem frightening as well as narrowly vindictive.

The judgement of the cross

In his letters to the Romans, and in the letter to the Colossians,[11] Paul picks up on the Old Testament understanding of wrath as part of judgement itself. In this sense, wrath becomes the reality of God's love, his anger at the effect of evil. When seen in this way, evil is not some sinister external force, but works in the human heart causing it to grow cold and eventually unable to either give or receive love. If judgement and wrath are to be understood as aspects of God's love at work, the cross faces us with the extent to which we have loved, or failed to love, one another as freely as God loves us. Christ does not simply substitute for human beings and he is not being punished in the way we normally understand punishment. He is meeting us in love in the place where sin hurts us most. This is true for both the victim and the perpetrator. He meets us where love has been given and then abused or rejected, as well as in the pain which comes with not being able to give or receive it.

> He meets us where love has been abused or rejected

This helps us to make sense of Paul's argument in his letter to the Romans where he speaks of Christ becoming a 'curse'. A person who broke the law to the extent of deserving the ultimate punishment was executed outside the city walls, becoming a curse in being alienated from the community. Christ takes on human shame as someone who is accursed. He identifies with what we least like about ourselves, so that he can meet us as we are.[12] He also meets us in our alienation, the sense of being an outsider or of not belonging, which is part of the experience of shame itself. In both of these situations, shame about who we are and alienation from others, Christ is, metaphorically speaking, taking on the human predicament as it is portrayed in the Adam and Eve story. But this still leaves us with the problem of sacrifice.

In what sense was Christ sacrificed for our sins?

Marcion, a theologian writing in the middle of the second century, who was later condemned as a heretic, attempted to come to terms with this question by concluding that the 'wrathful' God of the Old Testament had nothing to do with the God and Father of Jesus Christ. This led to his expurgation of large parts of the New Testament.[13] But Marcion's manipulation of Scripture only served to obscure the central meaning of the atonement.

In the religious world which Jesus inhabited, punishment for law-breaking was linked to the idea of sacrifice, and there were a number of different ways in which sacrifices could be made. One of these was the use of a goat as a representative of the guilty person or community. The people's sins were heaped on the goat, which was subsequently driven out of the camp. It carried the sins of the community and became 'alienated'.[14] There were also sacrificial payments, 'guilt' offerings in the form of grain or money given as a sign of repentance, as well as offerings of thanksgiving. Some sacrifices involved the ritual killing of animals and the spilling of their blood on the altar. While these seem abhorrent to us, they would have originally been inherited from the particular pagan culture context in which the early Hebrews lived. Most significantly, the blood which was spilled was thought to be the 'life' of the animal.[15]

One of the most important animal sacrifices, and it retains its symbolic meaning for both Jews and Christians today, was the slaughtering of the Paschal lamb. When Pharaoh refused to let God's people leave Egypt, God sent a plague to destroy every first-born male in Pharaoh's kingdom but promised to 'pass over' those houses of the Israelites whose lintels had been daubed with the blood of a lamb which had been sacrificed for that purpose. God commanded them to consume the flesh of the animal in haste before their departure from Egypt. The Paschal lamb was therefore both a symbol of God's mercy and a sign of deliverance. Christ himself embodies that mercy and in so doing becomes the 'instrument' of our deliverance from the destructive consequences of sin. But this still leaves us with the problem of how to interpret the meaning of his sacrifice without it becoming a symbol of a cruel and wrathful God who wills the sacrifice of his own Son.

The cross embodies the paradox of justice in a God who judges human beings through his mercy. From the cross, God sees human beings caught in a pattern of self-destruction. This is what we mean by the sinfulness of human nature.

> **God sees human beings caught in a pattern of self-destruction**

It is not that human beings are inherently bad, or that they should not be held to account for the deliberate harm they do to one another, but that God sees them as caught in an endless cycle of selfishness and violence which prevents them becoming what they were created to be, holy people confident in the knowledge of God's love. Holiness means being able to draw close to God unimpeded by guilt, the need to blame someone, and shame, despising or hating oneself. Christ is holy in himself and in his acceptance of human beings. He is holy in both his divine and human natures. The life which he gives in the blood shed on the cross makes peace by breaking down the walls of hostility which human beings create for themselves, and so enables them to participate in the very life of God.[16]

I hope that what I have said so far shows how the wrath of God, properly understood, is God's response to sin and to the destructive effect of sin, and not a demand for retribution in the form of sacrifice or punishment. When God's response to sin is only seen in punitive or substitutionary terms, Christ appears to be placating God and 'buying off' the death penalty due to those who break his law. In this

> Christ appears to be placating God

scenario, he *propitiates*, or appeases, God on our behalf. But this way of thinking about atonement has arisen out of a very partial understanding of the meaning of God's wrath.

If we are to speak of the wrath of God, we need to understand what causes it. Two considerations arise out of this question: the first, the motivating force behind God's decision to allow his Son to die, and the second, the nature of divine wrath itself. God's wrath is not directed at human beings, any more than a doctor tending a suffering child would be angry with the child. The doctor might feel anger about the circumstances which caused the suffering, such as war, poverty exacerbated by the effects of climate change, or the kind of bureaucracy and corruption which obstruct aid and medical help in disaster zones, but he or she would not feel angry with the child. The doctor's anger towards those who had contributed to the child's suffering corresponds to God's wrath as we see it described in parts of the Old Testament. His wrath is kindled by the greed and indifference of the wealthy towards the poor, as well as towards incompetent leaders who fail to take responsibility for their people and expose them to the danger of invasion.[17] He is not angry with the poor themselves. Similarly, the wrath of God is objective insofar as it is directed towards the *objective* issues of injustice and oppression, and it is *subjective* as the expression of outrage for the hurt which they cause to those he loves.[18]

Mercy and justice as the expression of wrath

This brings us to a third aspect of divine wrath, in addition to what motivates it and what form it takes, which has a crucial bearing on how we think of the work of atonement effected in Jesus Christ. It is, paradoxically, the mercy of God at work in his justice. This does not mean that God is soft on sin, but that his love makes justice re-creative rather than retributive. The atonement does not focus on punishment but on justice. The just judgement of the cross is God's response to the world's need of his love to reshape and re-invigorate every aspect of human existence. The life blood of Christ embodies God's mercy in delivering human beings from what Paul called the 'death' of sin, a death which blocks or destroys human potential and God's ongoing purpose for his world. Death is the evil which suffocates life and creativity. If God's love is inextricably bound up with the wrath he feels towards the cause of sin, he 'judges' sin by aligning himself with the sinner and at the same time sharing fully in the pain experienced by the victims of the sins of others. The cross declares the once and for all event of God's justice to be mediated in

> God's justice is mediated in a forward movement of reconciliatory love

a forward movement of reconciliatory love and not in a backward-looking revisiting of past sins in which nothing is learned for the future. Repentance consists in accepting the unconditional love of God given once and for all from the cross and in allowing that love to be the beginning of new life.

In judging sin from the cross, God is also effecting the ultimate judgement on evil. The desolation of Christ is a conflict with evil, the inverse or opposite of the ancient mythic conflicts between God and Baal or Marduk. These mythic conflicts involve active battle in which God conquers the enemy and brings order out of chaos. In the conflict of the cross God allows himself to lose the battle by being literally 'God forsaken', in order to win it by meeting human beings in their own desolation.

He is present to the exile which is part of the human predicament, as pictured in the Adam and Eve allegory of expulsion. At the heart of all exile situations is the question 'Why?', humanity's cry of incomprehension in the face of suffering. The primal cry which accompanies human birth is a cry of protest at the exile of life itself and will be repeated in that person's every attempt to make sense of separation and breakdown throughout his or her life. The 'why?' of the crucified

Christ contains, or holds, humanity's search for meaning in the context of suffering and, by doing so, restores the dignity and worth of those whose suffering goes unnoticed. In the cry of Jesus their suffering is 'comprehended' (as light 'comprehends', or 'overcomes', darkness at the beginning of John's Gospel) in the love of God, who redeems it from the chaos and non-being of evil.[19] Christ is 'forsaken' in the closed tomb and in his descent into what we call 'hell', for want of a better word to describe the depths of human desolation and the emotional and physical pain of despair. It is from this place that God confronts evil and effects atonement.

Christ judges sin in his reconciling of opposites, the divine and the human, the spiritual and material, heaven and earth, in the vertical and horizontal bars of the cross itself. The vertical represents the divine–human opposites, the heaven and earth dimension, and the horizontal, God embracing humanity in the outstretched arms of Christ. The cross symbolizes the bringing together of justice and mercy, which until now have seemed to be contradictory aspects of God's character. God's love now becomes the 'correlative' of his wrath.[20]

Atonement as expiation

It is in Christ that complete *expiation* of sin is made possible. God expiates sin in his love for human beings and transforms the human predicament into one which is *as if sin had never been*.[21] Julian of Norwich, in her book *Revelations of Divine Love*, speaks of the 'reparation' of sin and of God's judgement overwhelming the damage it causes: 'He taught me that I should see the glorious reparation, for this making of amends is incomparably more pleasing and honouring to God than ever was the sin of Adam harmful.'[22] Julian's thinking brings us back to the crucial difference between a *substitutionary* theory of atonement and ways of thinking about the atonement which stress the expiation of sin and the transformation of the human person. A substitutionary theory which emphasizes the punishment of Christ in our place says nothing about his full identification with human suffering, his *sumpatheo*, as he enters into our pain and experiences it in his God-forsakenness from within the effect of sin itself.

He suffers on a psychological and spiritual level, as well as on a physical one. It is in this sense that he 'becomes' sin by becoming as we are, *in order* that we may become as he is.[23] This presents a

> He 'becomes' sin by becoming as we are

very different picture of God from the one given by an exclusively substitutionary interpretation of atonement.

A partial view of atonement as both penal and substitutionary also distorts the meaning of justice itself. Biblical scholars and other theologians have argued that God's nature is one of justice and mercy, the one being the corollary of the other. In the Old Testament the altar of sacrifice was both the seat of judgement and the seat of mercy, and this is reflected both in the Deuteronomic law and in the Holiness Code. God is an impartial judge[24] who is, nevertheless, more inclined to be merciful than to punish, although he is by no means indifferent to sin.[25] The Christian understanding of atonement also connects us to the story of the exodus. In Christian theology, Christ is the lamb through whom God expiates, or effaces, sin itself. He is the 'Lamb of God who takes away the sin of the world'[26] along with the 'condemnation'[27] of guilt and shame which prevents human beings from becoming fully what they were created to be.

So what is repentance?

At the beginning of this book I said that finding someone to blame for our suffering helps to shift some of the pain, but, as with the shifting of any heavy load, this is only true in a very impermanent and superficial way. Shifting blame, or finding ways of prolonging a state of denial in regard to sin, does not supply the means or create the moral environment in which forgiveness and reconciliation can take place. Neither does punishment advance the healing process. When someone is given a lengthy prison sentence for a violent crime, the perceived justice meted out may briefly satisfy the victim and the general public, but ultimately does little to salve the hurt which the victim has experienced.

Nevertheless, the perpetrators of suffering do need to acknowledge the damage they have caused if they and their victims are to experience healing.[28] Forgiveness involves change and needs to be actively sought. I cannot expect to be forgiven if I have not indicated in some way that I would like forgiveness. In order to do this, I have to acknowledge the pain I have caused, or to which I may have contributed. There also has to be some kind of resolve not to repeat the wrong action and, where possible, to make good the damage.[29]

Without the perpetrator's desire for forgiveness, there is nowhere for that forgiveness to go and it is in this sense that the person who has been wronged 'retains' the sin.[30] At the same time, where sins, and forgiveness itself, are retained all parties experience ongoing pain, guilt or shame. We see this happening in the kind of dysfunctional family which avoids talking about significant and painful moments from the past. There is often a certain amount of collusion at work in this. In my own experience of visiting the elderly, and sometimes of helping a family prepare a funeral, I have encountered situations where people have 'forgotten' huge parts of their lives and nobody has dared help them remember. One lady I visited, who was known to have had a difficult relationship with her daughters, told me that she could not remember any of their childhood. The reason for this was

Some people 'forget' huge parts of their lives

that she was absent for most of it. Her way of 'not remembering' was a way of dealing with guilt. Some members of her family colluded with her 'amnesia' in view of her age and of the fact that it would be 'too cruel' to encourage her to speak of her failure as a parent and seek forgiveness from her children.

The process of forgiveness and healing involves helping one another to put down the burdens of guilt and shame. Where these burdens are not put down, successive generations inherit them in some form or other. People who have been abused in childhood often become abusers. The forgiveness process may have been interrupted or never have taken place, so that they 'retain' the burden of those sins and pass them on to their children.

Repentance also involves the remaking of relationships, on a national as well as a personal scale. Where the possibility for reconciliation is blocked by the build-up of distrust and hatred, the same hatred resurfaces later in history. International relations have broken down repeatedly as a result of old hatreds remaining buried and old sins unforgiven for several generations, only to re-emerge later in the vicious internecine conflicts of Rwanda and Bosnia, or former Yugoslavia, or in unresolved issues of justice relating to land, as in the conflict in Palestine–Israel. All of these situations point to a state of alienation, of being disconnected from one another.

Conclusion

So far, I have described how a Christian theory of atonement which is not restricted to penal substitution is at the heart of the reconciliation or 'at-one-ment' needed in every kind of broken relationship context, beginning with the relationship which exists between God and human beings. This at-one-ment is effected in the merciful judgement of the cross. The writer of the letter to the Colossians speaks of Christ 'making peace through the blood of his cross'.[31] The peace which Christ gives is not a withdrawal from the world or from the difficult questions raised by Scripture, but a peace which enables a going forward into the future, looking to break down the walls of human alienation. It is a hope-filled and dynamic way of living in God and in reconciliation with those who have been wronged by human sin, including the sins of society and of unjust systems and social structures so that it is also 'for the healing of the nations'.[32] The peace given by Christ in the 'life' of his blood is forgiveness itself. But in what sense is this forgiveness redemptive?

Part 2

MAKING SENSE OF REDEMPTION

4

The redemptive love of God

If Christ atoned for sin, what more is there left for God to do? If Christ has expiated what prevented reconciliation between God and human beings, surely this ought to mean that nothing more needs to be done?

In a sense, this is true. The atoning work of the cross brings people back to a position where they can begin all over again with God. A new deal, or covenant, exists between God and his people, something resembling a truce or treaty but which has infinitely greater implications. As with a treaty, it can only take effect when both parties move towards one another. When a person accepts what has been offered on the cross, the covenant is 'ratified' in the completion of a new relationship between that person and God. There is nobody else involved, although others may respond to God's invitation on behalf of a child at his or her baptism, when the child is publicly claimed for Christ and welcomed into the family of God. Adult baptism requires that a person declares his or her covenanted allegiance to Christ in the presence of the worshipping community, while parents and godparents do this on a child's behalf, and take responsibility for raising that child in the Christian faith until such time as he or she is able to make a personal declaration of faith at Confirmation. In both cases, God's redemptive love is given for that person as one who has been 'chosen' by God himself[1] but each person's decision to respond to that love is ultimately his or her own.

Finding new bearings – response and re-orientation to God

The new covenant between God and human beings involves a decision to 'turn back', or turn one's life around, so as to be once again 'fixed' on God in the way a ship 'fixes' or plots its course on a star. The New Testament Greek word for repentance is *metanoiea*, which means 'to turn around'. This turning around, or repenting, can be both personal and collective, a decision taken by a community, Church or nation to re-orientate its life according to the precepts of the kingdom of heaven. Furthermore, the decision to enter into this new relationship, or covenant, with God is one in which heart priorities take precedence over head priorities. The decision is governed by a renewed need for God's presence in a person's life, or in the life of a community, and for God's love to continually bring them back to their true selves. It is both rational and intuitive. In other words, sensing a real need for God is a logical conclusion made in the head but reached through the heart. This is only possible when we allow the rational part of us, our will, to be informed and graced by love for God and by the knowledge of his love for us.

Getting into a place of new relationship with God involves a simplicity of spirit which does not come easily to most of us. By simplicity of spirit I mean an unequivocal desire for God *for his own sake*. Desiring God for his own sake is the natural response to God's desire for every human being *for his or her own sake*, in the fullness of what a person was created to be. A parishioner once told me how this realization changed her life in a single moment. She was recalling a particular aspect of a very dysfunctional childhood during which she felt she did not belong in any of the home contexts which were being constructed around her. Her parents had separated when she was very young and her mother, a popular and beautiful socialite, moved to London. Georgia lived there with her step family but never felt she belonged. She was also sent abroad to spend time with her father, who usually hived her off on to other relatives, so that she felt she did not belong there either. One day, the au pair forgot to collect her from school. Georgia often finds herself reliving that time of waiting alone in a dark cloakroom with an irritated teacher complaining about her presence long after school had finished for the day. She experienced a profound and frightening sense of abandonment, as well as of shame, a sense that she had no right to exist at all and was an encumbrance to everyone wherever she was placed. She told me this story because later, when she had learned that God could be trusted with her memories, it was this particular experience of fear in abandonment, together with the dull realization of belonging to nobody in particular, which caused her to appreciate for herself the welcome God offers to people from the cross. Using the words of Psalm 22, 'My God, my God, why

> She appreciated for herself the welcome God offers to people from the cross

have you forsaken me?', a passage which Georgia later found very helpful, Christ honours us in our humiliation, from his own God-forsakenness.[2]

Being real with God – a painful healing

Understood in this way, the atoning work of Christ becomes both a healing and a reconciliatory event, but healing can be painful, and the judgement of mercy which is fully revealed as God's righteousness in his Son can also be painful. It obliges human beings to face their memories and to see the truth about themselves and about their relationships, especially when these have been in any way abusive. These kinds of painful memories distort reality when it comes to being real before God. They often require compensating delusions and fantasies which serve as coping mechanisms in a person's life, but which need to be exposed and healed by the redemptive love of God if that person is to become fully human, or fully the self God created him or her to be. Overemphasizing a propitiatory under-standing of atonement creates an imbalance in the way human beings think about themselves in relation to God. Not only are some people repelled by what seems like cruel vindictiveness on his part, but in some cases, as happened with the person quoted in Chapter 3, this understandable repulsion turns into a damaging form of self-hatred which makes it difficult for them to believe that they deserve God's love. Believing themselves to be undeserving brings a defensive, and sometimes hostile, reaction to God's invitation to be at one with him. As a result, they step away from him, rather than towards him. There is no basis for trust in such a fearful situation, so that there is neither the means nor the incentive for change. Why, after all, should someone want to have anything to do with such a God, let

> There is neither the means nor
> the incentive for change

alone seek his help in understanding and forgiving oneself?

When the Christian understanding of atonement is seen in purely retributive terms, these will be reflected in a similarly narrow and conditional understanding of God's redemptive love, both of which derive from a misunderstanding of his justice. As I said in Chapter 3, God's justice and his mercy are expressed in his 'wrath', the indignation he feels in the oppression and suffering of the most vulnerable. Mercy and justice are also two aspects of God's righteousness, what is called in Hebrew *tsedeq*. They are the two facets of his character as a righteous God, the one completing the other. His mercy *is* his justice and his justice *is* his mercy. If God's justice is revealed in his mercy, the judgement handed down from the cross becomes God's ultimate act of forgiveness and acceptance of human beings as and where they are in the moment of their turning back, their *metanoiea*. This is what Paul means when he says that it was 'while we still were sinners [that] Christ died for us'.[3] It tells us that there is nothing we can do to make God love us more, and that there is nothing we can do to make him love us less.

Starting from where we are

This means that God loves us for who we are, despite what we do to ourselves. In meeting every human person in that individual's darkest place, God makes it possible for a new encounter to begin, one in which suffering and sin have been overwhelmed by his love. This is what John means when he describes Christ as the light which 'shines in the darkness, and the darkness did not overcome it'.[4] God's love overwhelms each person's darkness, whether past or present, from the cross, in order to allow for new growth to begin from what has been spoiled in our lives.

The once and for all event of the cross opens the way for the redemptive love of God to begin working in a new way from this place. But all new beginnings, especially where human relationships are concerned, need something or someone to prompt or make the first move. In a dispute, even though both parties may want to be reconciled, one or other needs to take the initiative in order for reconciliation to begin. God takes this initiative himself. The cross becomes the 'meeting place' for God and humanity. The centurion standing at the foot of the cross realizes this in his declaration that 'Truly this man was God's Son.'[5] Human response to God's initiative begins in the moment of 'turning' towards Christ and sensing his presence from within our own darkness. We start from where we are and 'feel our way' towards redemption.

Repentance: feeling the need

But what is it that we are being redeemed *from*? And what does redemption feel like? The New Testament Greek word for sin is *hamartia*, a term which was usually employed in the context of archery, signifying to miss or fall short of the mark. In Chapter 2 the problem of sin was examined in a largely social context, but the way in which sin works to disfigure and destroy our humanity, through structures and systems, makes falling short of the mark seem rather inadequate as an illustration of this kind of sin. There are cosmic and literary comparisons we could make with the word *hamartia* – bits of the universe pursuing an endless trajectory into some deeper darkness, perhaps – but this still does not provide a realistic picture of sin as we know it in our times and contextual circumstances, or of its devastating effects. Nor does it seem to trigger any sense of lack or need.

When we speak of redemption from sin we are really looking to fill a certain sense of loss or meaninglessness. I was once travelling down Oxford Street on the top deck of a bus and was suddenly struck by the emptiness of that place, despite the thousands of people and the shops and buildings. I sensed a need, not only in myself but in all the people around me, for an awareness of some greater purpose, a wider field of vision and a need to begin again from that moment. I think this was a call to the kind of repentance which leads to redemption, a redemption which brings us to a new place of understanding the human predicament in relation to God.

The Greek words for both sin and repentance, as they are employed by Paul, provide a lead into their meaning and purpose for our own times. Paul speaks of *apolutrosis*, a word meaning 'to buy back' or 'redeem', in the sense that an article placed with a pawnbroker can be redeemed for a certain price. In Paul's view, human beings have literally been 'bought back' in the blood of Christ. While this may provide a theological connection between the 'life blood' of sacrifice and the sacrifice of Christ, we have already seen that sacrificial language is not always helpful when it comes to making sense of atonement for today. It also makes repentance seem somewhat mechanical, involving some form of commercial transaction to put things back on course. We need, therefore, to rediscover a concept of sin as one which involves acting and thinking in the interests of a travesty of the individual's true self. The same is true with regard to our manipulation and domination of other people's true selves. Being 'bought back' from this situation involves, first of all, the will or desire for change, as we saw in connection with forgiveness, and second, the desire for God himself, for his own sake.

The way we think about redemption is therefore closely connected to the way we think about God and his atoning work in Jesus Christ and with the way we eventually come to be reconciled with ourselves. Emphasizing substitutionary theories of atonement and representative sacrifice associated with guilt and shame is a sign that many Christians have only known a God whom it is impossible to please. Thinking about atonement in these terms also suggests that human beings are entirely passive in matters of reconciliation and redemption. We have already seen that fearing God does not mean being afraid of him, any more than respecting a parent or teacher prevents us from loving him or her. Fear disrupts relationship because it paralyses love. It makes us believe that love has to be earned and therefore deserved, as in the kind of dysfunctional family relationship in which children feel they need to be constantly performing well in order to please their parents and earn their love. A punishment and reward scenario, whatever form it takes, does not provide the conditions needed for change and growth into new life. In fact, it does quite the opposite. In generating fear, the threat of punishment or the promise of some arbitrary reward defeats trust before it has had a chance to take root, and trust is the basis for redemption.

Learning trust

Trust in God is the essence of faith. It derives from an expiatory understanding of atonement (the effacing of sin in Christ's complete solidarity with the human condition) and prepares the way for a participatory understanding of redemption itself. Christian redemption means belonging once again in God through Christ. Belonging in and to God comes with vulnerability to God, a loving and confident response to Christ's own vulnerability to human violence on the cross. When human beings allow themselves to trust, in being vulnerable to God's love, Christ begins the mending of that state of fundamental alienation which exists between them, as well as between them and God's world. As we saw in the Adam and Eve story, the damage begins from the moment we become conscious beings, from the moment we are aware of the implications of our freedom to make choices. But limiting the Christian idea of atonement and redemption to a narrow interpretation of the Adam and Eve story, and to disobedience and punishment, constrains its meaning and so makes it difficult for people to connect Christ's suffering and dying with their own life experience, with their need to relearn trust and with the suffering of the world.

> **The damage begins from the moment we are aware of the implications of choice**

The disobedience and punishment rationale may provide a limited description of the human situation, but my own experience as a university chaplain has shown it to be far from helpful when it comes to meeting people where they are in life's journey and in the questions and difficulties raised by today's politics, ethics and social mores. Neither does it help them to develop a spirituality which will sustain them now and into the future. What is needed is a new way of thinking about the redemptive work of God in Jesus Christ which allows for a complementarity between the rational and the deeper life of the spirit.

Christ's solidarity with the human condition allows us to think of the meaning and purpose of human existence in an entirely new way, one which is beyond the rational, but which also informs the rational. Much of the controversy surrounding the issue of faith and its place in modern secular life derives from a misunderstanding of the nature of faith itself. Faith begins when the grace given in the redemptive love of God transforms the individual and human intelligence itself. It makes what the Bible calls Wisdom. Wisdom leads to understanding, which in turn enables human beings to be 'in step' with God, to keep his laws.[6] Confidence in our belonging together in the love of God is the product of that faith. But how do we speak of a faith which is grounded in this kind of confidence to the parents of a terminally ill child? And how relevant is it to the suffering of innocent people caught up in war or environmental disaster? It seems as if, for all that is said about redemption, the unpredictability of the world and the fickleness of human nature remain unchanged. On the whole, this is not surprising, as human understanding relies predominantly on human intelligence to make sense, if at all possible, of the incomprehensible. But faith which is rooted in trust is shaped at a much deeper level, one which allows us to say, like Job in his darkest moments, 'I know that my Redeemer lives.'[7] This is neither blind belief nor arrogant conviction. It is the knowledge of Wisdom which leads to understanding. Job meets God in the darkness. We meet God in the desolation of the cross and we celebrate our belonging together in that place and in the risen life of his Son. The paradox of repentance is therefore one of celebration.

Needing one another – the making of a new sociality

Meeting God in the darkness and in the desolation of the cross helps us to make sense of the purpose of the suffering and dying of Christ and of how this purpose continues to work itself out in our relationships. It relates, once again, to how we think about sin and shame. Earlier, I said that the disobedience of Adam and Eve is a way of talking about human beings no longer feeling they need God. Their disobedience consists in denying that need. They want to 'own' or control their own destiny. This creates a rupture in the fabric of human relations in which short-term benefit to the individual, or to a particular interest group, comes with the desire for power which in turn drives the political process. In the life of the Church, as well as in that of governments and industries, power-driven agendas pay little attention to the real human needs of those they are there to serve.[8] Imagine how differently the economic challenges of today would have been met if Wisdom had dictated the decision-making processes of banks and those of the rich and powerful.

This is perhaps to dream of Utopia, but it also points to a deeper reality, one which is grounded in the love of God and in people's need for trust in all human relationships. The two needs are bound up with one another. Holding them in tension with the real and practical needs which must be addressed in political and administrative processes allows us to see human history, as well as the future, in an entirely different way.[9] Metaphorically, human beings have become individuals in disconnecting themselves from a loving God and from a deeper and more compassionate mutuality with other creatures, and in assuming a sovereignty over the earth which is easily corrupted by human greed and selfishness. Redemption challenges the sovereignty of the individual in the offering of the kind of forgiveness which can rework this situation. What I have said about belonging together in Christ challenges the individual to become a true self, a full person conscious of his or her worth in the eyes of God and of his love for the world. It is the beginning of genuine sociality.

> Imagine if Wisdom had dictated the decision-making processes of banks

Confidence in God's love runs counter to a marketing–consumerist culture. Consumerism thrives on the basis that it is possible to persuade anyone about anything which is likely to improve how they feel about themselves. If what I have said so far about the way we experience shame is true, persuading people that they can feel better about themselves is not necessarily a bad thing. The problem comes when shame and low self-esteem are used to persuade people to buy products which promise what is not in their power to deliver. As a general example, television and internet advertising for cars, clothes and cosmetics operates on the basis of a tacit understanding between advertisers and consumers in which the consumers, if persuaded, will respond to a blurring of the truth about themselves as persons. In other words, advertising relies on fantasy in order to achieve its desired ends. Fantasy is not in itself bad unless it leads to unmanageable debt and the kind of anxiety which comes with the disintegration of a person's inner life and sense of contingency with the world and society. Ironically, advertisers want to persuade the individual that he or she is unique and valuable, but valuable to whom? And why?[10] These questions return to us unanswered, from a spiritual vacuum.

Paradoxically, they also reveal something about what the redemptive work of Christ is about. When consumers become entirely enmeshed in fantasy they are in fact experiencing shame. The more things we use to hide from ourselves, the more things we need to keep the fantasy going, and to hide not only from ourselves, but from others and from God. Hiding also takes other forms. Alcohol and work addiction, to name but two, reveal a similar pattern. Both of these areas of addiction allow people to hide from themselves, from those closest to them, and from God. As in the Genesis story, hiding from their true selves is a sign that they 'know that they are naked'. My own experience of alcoholic parents has taught me that this is why addicted people often find it very hard to receive love.

Addiction of every kind means that a human being, who is unique in the eyes of God, is now owned by what that person consumes, so that he or she is no longer in a position to make free choices. Free choices are not limited to shopping. They affect all human relationships.[11] A person who is not free with regard to the choices he or she makes also finds it difficult to be free towards others in the giving and receiving of love, an exchange which depends on trust. People who cannot trust enough to receive love also find it hard to give love in a way which does not either manipulate the receiver, by inducing guilt, or expect a return on their investment in a desire to 'own' the other person. The nineteenth-century theologian Friedrich Schleiermacher describes this syndrome as a *spiritual* malaise which is the root cause of selfishness, the most destructive element of the human condition.

Schleiermacher argues that there are two opposing forces at work in a person's psyche, the need to protect the self and the desire to be in solidarity with others.[12]

> Two opposing forces are at work – self and solidarity with others

In selfish or abusive relationships neither person is free, and freedom is at the heart of the Christian understanding of redemption.

Paul writes that it is 'for freedom' that 'Christ has set us free',[13] so that the gift of redemption is in fact a liberation from every kind of bondage, or what Paul calls 'slavery to sin'. Those who are free do not need to use other people to protect them from the truth about themselves, since their freedom derives from knowing their true worth in the eyes of a loving God who has made each one for himself. St Augustine, in his *Confessions*, describes how this realization of God's purpose and love for every human being motivates prayer and makes worship a vital necessity.[14] The redemption offered by Christ is the gift of reconciliation with God and the freedom which comes with it, and the dynamic forward movement of loving reconciliation in human relationships is a sign of that freedom.

Being brought home – from alienation to reconciliation

In his book *The Courage to Be*, the theologian Paul Tillich speaks of the courage it takes to become human from within a person's deeper centre which only God can fully understand.[15] Faith is forged within this deep centre and is continually being 'worked' in and through that person by the action of God's redemptive grace.[16] This is part of God's ongoing creative work, in which he is 'reconciling the world to himself'.[17] The redemptive process is God's reconciling of human beings with their true selves and with one another. Seen in these terms, Christian redemption begins with the realization of our need for God as one who in Christ suffers *with* us.[18] In his acceptance of suffering, Christ is taking responsibility for the whole human race.[19]

He does this in his own freedom. Earlier, I said that taking responsibility for another is not the same as being culpable. Culpability focuses on guilt and on punishment in which the offender is a passive recipient of blame. Responsibility involves, as the word implies, an active 'response' to a situation. Christ's redemptive act is therefore a loving response to the alienated human condition. It is a forward movement, a new encounter, initiated by God himself and illustrated in the story of the prodigal son.[20] The story is more complex and layered than it might at first seem. It is not only about a repentant younger son. It is also about a father who sees him in the distance and is already running towards him to bring him home, long before the son has reached the gates of his father's house. One might imagine the father going to find the son before he has even set off for home, in the moment that he decides to return.

Redemption begins where people are, not where they wish they could be, or think they should be. This is also true for those who are victims of other people's sin. The story told to me by Georgia, of her sense of abandonment and loneliness in the moment of being forgotten at school, evokes a little of what we feel when, as victims of other people's sin, we need to be found by God. It speaks to the lostness which so many experience in the low points of their lives. In these moments, God embraces those who have been wronged, as he embraces the ones who have caused their suffering from the moment the perpetrator owns his or her need for forgiveness. He visits human beings in their alienation, as victims and as perpetrators of suffering, and begins to repair the damage we do to ourselves from there.

This forward movement of reconciliation involves the whole of Christ's life. It begins in the moment of his incarnation in which God literally waits on the acceptance of human beings to be reconciled, to be put right or 'justified' with God through their faith in Jesus Christ. In her 'yes' to the angel, Mary allows that redemptive process to begin. In one of his homilies, St Bernard of Clairvaux describes this moment as the whole of creation waiting on her courageous acquiescence to all which God's redemptive act in Christ will demand of her:

> The angel awaits an answer; it is time for him to return to God who sent him. We too are waiting, O Lady, for your word of compassion . . . The price of our salvation is offered to you. We shall be set free at once if you consent.[21]

Here we have the suggestion of a new beginning already being shaped by God from within the contingency of human history. It tells us that God in Christ is redeeming, or in this sense rescuing, humanity from itself. So there is a re-orientation, a fetching back of the human race in this moment of incarnation in which the redemptive word of God, his invitation to reconciliation, is completed, or ratified, in a woman's answering 'yes'. God is now in solidarity with human beings in order that human beings might participate fully in his life.

Participation in God

What I have said so far in this book suggests that participation in God's own life is part of his original redemptive purpose. In terms of Adam and Eve's metaphorical exile, participating in God's life reconnects human beings with God and with the whole of creation. They are brought home, and in being 'back home' they begin to experience a real transformation from within what Paul calls 'the spirit'. Desires, the ambitions and material 'must haves' of modern life, are transformed as the greater needs of the human spirit begin to be recognized.

In his conversation with the Samaritan woman, Jesus reveals this transformative process at work.[22] Having been initially astonished that Jesus knows 'everything that [she has] ever done', and that he could, she imagines, provide her with an unlimited supply of fresh water without her having to fetch it in a bucket, the woman begins to realize the true significance of his words. Her past is not what matters most to him and the water of which he is speaking, though unlimited, quenches a different kind of thirst, the thirst of the human spirit for God. She is also amazed, as were the disciples, that he is talking to her, since she is not only a woman but a Samaritan. Women were completely marginalized and Samaritans

> The water of which he is speaking quenches a different kind of thirst

were considered to have apostatized from the Jewish faith by intermarrying with Canaanites and other foreigners, so she was 'impure' in both respects. She was alienated socially, as well as from the religious milieu of her time. But Jesus affirms her both as a woman, by respecting her questions (in fact this is one of the most profound theological conversations in the Gospels), and as a Samaritan. He is also creating a level playing field between Samaritans and Jews when it comes to where either group should worship. He tells her that temples and mountains and, by implication, churchmanship and denominations, are not what matter to God. What matters most to God is the recognition that we have spiritual needs which are greater than the material things which concern us, because it is in the spiritual life that the truth about the human predicament is first discerned.

Conclusion

The conversation which Jesus has with the Samaritan woman reveals God's involvement with human beings in his gift of redemptive life, the life, death and resurrection of his Son. Participating in God's life leads to a new form of dynamic existence for those who are now made one 'in God', a life which is continually moving and shaping itself around times and circumstances, and which reveals hope. The next chapter will look at how Christians respond, and sometimes fail to respond, to God's invitation to participate in this life and in his redemptive work in the world.

5

Ongoing redemption

Do we have to earn redemption? Does God have favourites?
Is God really free? Is there such a thing as destiny? What is
the Church and what is it for?

What I have said so far about the nature of redemption still leaves
us with questions. For one thing, the word 'redemption' is itself
problematic. Not only does the Greek *apolutrosis* suggest that some
sort of commercial transaction, or deal, is taking place between
God and human beings, it also hints at a certain partiality, that God
has 'favourites'. The belief that God's love is conditional and that his
primary concern is for the 'predestined' or 'saved' individual remains
one of the underlying causes of division among Christians today.
It also causes a good deal of confusion surrounding the meaning of
the word 'redemption' itself. First, because predestination resonates
with the idea of fate, so that it seems that Christian teaching could
be confused or conflated with certain forms of Hinduism, in which
Karma and past lives dictate a person's present existence, as well as
with certain Buddhist teachings also relating to reincarnation and
enlightenment. Second, predestination can also imply that the power
of fate, or destiny, in some way dictates what God chooses to do,
so that God does not seem to be
altogether free in his own choices.
If God is not free, how can he create
human beings who are free to choose
whether or not to willingly engage
with his transforming grace?

> If God is not free, how can
> he create human beings who
> are free to choose?

When Martin Luther nailed his Ninety-Five Theses to the door of
the castle church of Wittenburg in 1517 he did so in the conviction
that freedom is God's supreme and unconditional gift to anyone who
places his or her faith in Jesus Christ. The redemptive work of the

cross consists in freedom from guilt and from the need to earn God's love. Faith in Jesus Christ is the means whereby that work begins to take effect in the lives of human beings. Luther's action, and the teaching which followed, is thought by most scholars to have started the Protestant Reformation by challenging the right of the Church[1] to impose conditions on salvation. Division and dissent have continued to dissipate the life of the Church since Luther's declaration, and thereby to compromise the truth of the gospel it preaches, but the spirit of what Luther said remains a central truth for Christians today. It means that the love of God, and his free gift of grace to all who turn to him and receive it takes precedence over the right of any Church or interest group to pass judgement on another Christian, or to place conditions for his or her membership within the Christian family. Luther's declaration of God's free gift of grace did not always develop in this spirit, but it did allow for a renewed understanding of forgiveness. His declaration of justification by faith means that people are once again put in a right relationship with God from the moment they want this to happen and for as long as they trust in the forgiveness proffered from the cross. In being justified by faith they receive the freedom which comes with forgiveness, the kind of freedom we experience when an angry scene or a long-term dispute with a partner or close family member is resolved. There is a moment of complete freedom, of 'lightness of being', in which anything good and creative becomes possible, so that the freedom which comes with reconciliation is essentially creative. Where there is reconciliation and forgiveness the freedom which it brings removes the constraints and conditions which prevent the redemptive work of God's ongoing presence taking effect in the life of the Church.

> **Division and dissent have continued to dissipate the life of the Church**

For freedom Christ has set us free[2]

Today, Luther's idea that a person is put in right relationship with God solely on the basis of trust challenges denominational exclusivity and the idea that membership of the Church is in some way conditional. It also challenges the right of any one group to appropriate truth and to distort it into immovable absolutes in a literal and unquestioning way of reading the Bible. Real faith frees the intellect. In fact it requires that we continually move on intellectually, asking the kind of questions which keep Christians in touch with secular society, without viewing it as an enemy to be either conquered or appeased. Christians are called to think intelligently from within a living relationship with God, believing in the goodness of society and in his love for it. A healthy intellect keeps faith alive and makes for compassion in the life of the Church and in its witness to the world.

Many people are put off going to church because it does not help them connect in a compassionate and intelligent way with the world or with God himself. They find it either boring or superficial, more about getting a religious buzz than supplying the means to live out the freedom promised in Christ. They also cannot understand why churches alienate or exclude certain people, or why mission seems to be designed to get people into the building but afterwards provides little to help them travel deeper in their spiritual life, or give them the intellectual freedom they need to explore life's difficult questions in the context of their faith. Some of the people I have spoken to also find church dull because it feels spiritually inert. Others have found that in certain churches they encounter the opposite in a spirituality which feels 'hyper'. Too much emotion is flying around and this can be intimidating and make newcomers feel inadequate. There seem to be different kinds of expectations to be met in each of these contexts and it all feels very controlling.

In Jesus, we see a God who has no desire to control or exclude people. Jesus stood against the kind of narrow legalism which stunts human development in his challenging of the religious experts of his day, especially those who enforced rules and regulations which they ignored themselves. Today, many

> **In Jesus, we see a God who has no desire to control or exclude people**

people who are leaving their church do so either because they have outgrown its narrow and authoritarian theology and social ethics, or because the formality of its worship and the banality of its preaching fail to connect with their lives in any meaningful way. When I was training for ordination, one of our tutors would preface his critique of our sermons with the simple question, 'Where's the good news of the gospel in all this?' His words ring in my ears every time I preach. The gospel is good news when it is read prayerfully and when sermons have been prepared intelligently from within the inner space of a person's life with God. The preached word then becomes sacramental and stands a better chance of meeting people's need to experience God's word for themselves and be resourced by it for the coming week.

The problem of spiritual under-resourcing is made worse in a prevailing climate of church activism in which mission plans formed at management level, but seldom shaped in the silence of prayer, leave little time or mental space for the pastoral care and spiritual nurture of the people, or of their clergy. By activism I mean the kind of activities undertaken either because the diocese has agreed on a strategy for church growth, with goals and objectives linked to numbers and parish quotas, or because of an increasing sense that churches need to justify their existence in the face of secular doubt and cynicism. This puts a great deal of pressure on clergy, as well as on a few dedicated lay people. It is difficult for these churches to supply a sensitive and intelligent rationale for believing in God, or the confidence needed for people to entrust their lives to him, because they are too busy meeting other people's agendas.[3]

Peter Kendall, a former Methodist, describes the problem in these terms:

> Institutions often get [their] purposes diverted, because they create other agendas, because the people in them are in competition for power and whatever . . . Ideas become less important than the survival of the institution . . . I had doubts about the institutional delivery of an idea.[4]

These remarks, and those of many people I have spoken with, suggest a disillusionment with the Church as a whole. They see the Church as an organization which is trying to manage its way out of spiritual poverty. Church growth and mission are not invariably the same thing. The spiritual impoverishment of church life compromises its freedom to witness truthfully to the faith it is supposed to be celebrating and which should resource its care of people, both inside and outside its doors.

Radical hospitality and the meaning of mission

The gift of freedom which comes with a properly nurtured faith enables Christians to help others make sense of modern life. Christ's redemptive and re-creative work therefore supplies meaning and purpose to the work of Christian mission. In being a forgiven people Christians become bearers of hope. Freedom conveys hope when the redemptive work of Christ is visible in people's lives, its priority being the well-being of the human person and the radical welcome proffered to the outsider. The Church's mission ought therefore to be aimed at giving people back their humanity, a humanity which is often compromised by the demands of modern life, without requiring that they immediately join a church and without making excessive demands on their time and energy if they do.

Mission is about the offer of radical and unconditional hospitality, and it is here that the more sacramental denominations and churches have much to offer. The Eucharist, so beautifully described in George Herbert's poem 'Love', is about the celebration of God's hospitable love in the kind of unaffected

> **Mission is about the offer of radical and unconditional hospitality**

thanksgiving (the word 'eucharist' means 'to give thanks') which allows us to accept and love ourselves as we are. The sacramental grace which comes with the Eucharist allows people to accept those things which disfigure and distort their personhood, that which God fully knows about them and loves, however unattractive they may feel themselves to be:

> Love bade me welcome: yet my soul drew back,
> Guiltie of dust and sinne.
> But quick-ey'd love, observing me grow slack
> From my first entrance in,
> Drew nearer to me, sweetly questioning,
> If I lack'd anything.[5]

At the heart of the Eucharist there is a kind of silent space in which the spirit of God's loving acceptance of the whole Church is also at work. It is in this eucharistic silence that the Church, present as the worshipping community, finds the grace it needs to be a sign of reconciliation and hope. Grace empowers it to make a difference in a particular locality and to draw those it serves into the kingdom of heaven without expecting anything in return. When it offers a radical welcome to all people, irrespective of sexuality, gender or nationality, a church is pushing out the boundaries of the kingdom of heaven so as to embrace all of its surroundings. In so doing it bears the atoning work of Christ into the world.

The problem of identity

This only sounds idealistic when we forget that the cross is an at-one-ment event in which human beings are enabled, as a forgiven people, to participate in the life of God and to enter into his salvation work.[6] The problem comes when this work is compromised by concerns relating to identity. Having an identity means signalling that you are a 'something' or a 'someone' who is different, but who at the same time 'belongs' within a particular identity group. Some of these identities relate to churchmanship or to clergy or leadership status within a particular denomination. Others are issue-based and cross-denominational. These will often reflect a particular way of reading Scripture and of thinking about atonement and redemption and as a result can be extremely divisive. A number of people I spoke to when I was a university chaplain described how they left churches because they were told that their relationship with someone who was presumed to be a 'non-Christian' meant that they were 'mismatched'.[7] In one such case, the presumed 'non-Christian' was simply trying to explore his faith in a wider intellectual context than that which was permissible within the narrow theological confines of his worshipping community.

The word 'Christian' has become a defining identity in its own right which, until recently, was simply another way of describing oneself as Evangelical.[8] Nowadays, different Christian identities within the Church are usually forged within a form of systemization linked to subjective beliefs surrounding the most contentious issues of the time. Currently, and allowing for some cross-over on certain issues, church identities (Catholic and Protestant) derive from the disputes of the Reformation and are focused into churchmanships whose members may in turn identify themselves with different interest groups. These include being 'for' or 'against' the ordination of women to the priesthood and the episcopate, and 'for' or 'against' the ordination of gay people in practising relationships, to name but two.[9] Issue-driven politics create further divisions in the organizational life of the wider Church, which is already preoccupied with hierarchy and pragmatic decision-making. Not surprisingly, many people who love Christianity and the gospel are put off by the wrangles in the Church. They see it as an impersonal, and often unkind, organization with systems and controls like any other, and leave.[10]

F. D. Maurice, the nineteenth-century theologian who captured the unique spirit of Anglicanism, argued that the Church should be a spiritual society before anything else. The quality and depth of its prayer would then shape its moral decisions and order its politics, giving it a distinctive identity as a spiritual body in the secular world. Today, we are seeing the reverse of this, in a spiritual life which has become sidelined by the pressures of administration. This makes for frustration within the administrative and governing processes themselves and alienates clergy from those in authority because it undermines trust. Ever-increasing administrative loads encroach on the time needed for prayer and study and this makes for stressed and unhappy clergy. In being ill-resourced spiritually and intellectually, they find pastoral work particularly demanding, and pastoral casualties result. The people they want to serve then feel neglected, which in turn feeds a general dis-

> **Prayer would then shape its moral decisions and order its politics**

trust of the Church by those who think of themselves as Christian but remain outside its walls, along with a growing sense of alienation for many of those who remain steadfastly within them.[11]

Belonging but not belonging

Alienation makes love impossible because it generates distrust. John the Evangelist writes in his first letter that 'perfect love casts out fear'.[12]

He is speaking about the fear of punishment which corresponds to the guilt and shame which many people carry around for most of their lives, and which is often sown in childhood in circumstances they may not even remember. The Evangelist goes on to say that 'whoever fears has not reached perfection in love'. For us, this translates as 'fear makes it impossible to love, or to receive love', and this applies to all human relationships, including those in the life of the Church. Human beings are honoured and justified in a relationship with God which is built on mutual trust. God actually trusts us to be fully what he created us to be, not by our own efforts but in and through our love for him. In other words, God's purpose consists in a destiny which is dependent on the willingness of human beings to allow God's love to work through them into the lives of others. God's love for human beings therefore extends beyond identity and individualism. They are loved in their sociality, a sociality which is formed in relatedness to others and to God's creation.[13]

A person experiences a sense of diminishment when this relatedness is interrupted or spoiled, in separation and relationship breakdown and in manipulative 'shaming' relationships with close adults. Being diminished in this way makes it more difficult for that person to feel worthy of God's love and to experience a sense of belonging *with* others, rather than *to* others. Similarly, and as I suggested in the last chapter, the freedom promised to us in Christ is compromised when human beings are reduced to consumers. We are less than we were created to be as persons when we are in abusive relationships or when we are being manipulated by profit motives.

An implicit consumerism combined, paradoxically, with a concern for a purity which excludes certain people is part of the growth incentive in many churches. People feel alienated in being excluded from a church or group because of *what* they are, as opposed to being welcomed and accepted because of *who* they are. The problem of exclusion, especially as it relates to purity, goes back to the doctrine of predestination which still influences many Christians today.[14] The way in which it has been interpreted through the centuries has created a judgemental climate in which people

> The problem of exclusion goes back to the doctrine of predestination

assume they can tell if a person is a Christian on the basis of whether or not that person conforms to certain moral and theological absolutes, and, as I said earlier, these absolutes derive from the way in which Christians understand atonement and redemption and read the Bible. In each of these contexts for thinking about God's dealing with human beings lies a choice between two ways of living out the Christian faith and of belonging within a Christian community. The one defines a 'safe belief space' and offers security and a clear sense of belonging within a group of like-minded people. The other invites a deeper and more intuitive approach to Christian doctrine and to Scripture which encourages a sense of being part of a bigger picture in which Christians pattern their lives on Christ by entering more deeply into the world's suffering and into its need for God. In being present to the world in this way, through unbiased listening and what Paul calls genuine love,[15] Christians can be drawn ever more deeply into the relational nature of the redemptive love of God. They experience the life of the Trinity as a movement of exchange, an unspoken dialogue of compassion with the other, even those they dislike or with whom they disagree.

Learning love in the Church

Living the Christian faith from a place of compassion and vulnerability involves risk. First, because it rules out infallibility, whether of the Bible or of the authority vested in any one person or powerful ruling body. Second, because it involves the willingness to change the way we think by becoming less passive and unquestioning. Christians need to love the Church into a new place with their minds and hearts. Learning to love the Church requires that we challenge its failures and at the same time have compassion for it in the hurt it causes itself. Compassion poses a theological challenge to everyone. Participating in God's redemptive life requires that theology be continually relearned and then reworked in every church context, by the individual and the community, within the moving context of history, the individual's and the community's, and within the circumstances of particular social, political and ethnic environments.

Participating in God's redemptive life in all of these contexts shapes and identifies the Christian community, which is what the Church is supposed to be. The extent to which a local church visibly participates in God's life will depend on the extent to which it re-orientates itself to receiving his love. This is the re-orientation to repentance which I described in the last chapter. Its re-orientation to God 'defines' that community as a forgiven people. It acquires a new identity which reflects the infinite possibilities for truth, generated from within God's love, and which will reveal the working of God's mercy and justice in its common life.

Holding on to party preferences and beliefs which exclude people from a church suggests that we do not altogether trust God to do this transforming work for us himself. This in turn gives the impression that we are afraid that he might fail to be either just or merciful, depending which side of a dispute

> We do not trust God to do this transforming work for us himself

one takes, and there is seldom any question of giving others the benefit of the doubt. Also, the idea that any one denomination or interpretation of Scripture is the only way, and therefore the only truth, implies that God's love is itself conditional. One of the greatest obstacles to reconciliation in the Church is the idea that some people are saved and others are not. Different parties and denominations within the Church believe that only *their* particular understanding of truth and salvation is valid, although they will occasionally join forces to attack what they perceive as 'liberalism', seen as a syncretistic 'pick and choose' rationalization of the Christian life and a compromise with secular values and sexual mores.

The sixteenth-century lawyer and theologian Richard Hooker allowed for rational thought to interpret, and not simply analyse, both Scripture and tradition. In so doing, he introduced a 'middle way' which would allow opposite factions in the Church of England to live together. The use of the intuitive and the rational in the service of theology was not new in Hooker's time, but it had not been used to create a theology of the Church which would stabilize its life and heal the divisions of the Reformation. These divisions continue today. They run along the old fault lines of Protestant and Catholic, and of word and sacrament. They also pertain to a fundamental disagreement with respect to the meaning of atonement and redemption in regard to human destiny, free will and rational thought.

This is a complex subject, but what I have said so far in this book suggests that, in Jesus, God is alongside human beings in all of their rational choices. They are free to make those choices and are not controlled by him, or by some other supernatural force. But this still leaves us wondering about destiny. To what extent does God know and decide everything from the start? Exclusive and excluding ideas about atonement and redemption make this a difficult question to answer. Requiring that people accept penal substitution, or propitiatory atonement, as well as the infallibility of Scripture, or of the Church's teaching on specific issues, as conditions for membership of a church or group, constrains a person's freedom to make intellectual as well as moral choices. Furthermore, if our choices are also pre-ordained they are not really choices. In all of these cases, divine grace, and by implication the love of God, are made conditional and exclusive. They are destined for the select few. This kind of thinking has generated a climate of suspicion in the life of the Church and has led to separation, exclusion and a two-class system (the saved and the unsaved) which contradicts the gospel's central message of reconciliation and peace.

The controversy which caused the first major schism within Christianity, and which dominated the life of the Church for almost five hundred years, concerned the nature of God and the divinity and co-eternity of Christ and the Holy Spirit with the Father. But differences within the Church also derive from the way Christians have thought, and continue to think, about human destiny in relation to God. Some of these are closely associated with the doctrine of predestination. According to this doctrine, originally conceived by Martin Luther and further developed by John Calvin, God already knows the ultimate course of every human life and has already decided on its outcome. For Calvin, it is pre-ordained by his inscrutable and absolute will and by his justice, although his teaching also emphasized God's mercy in the 'assurance' of salvation to all who turned to Christ.[16] For both Luther and Calvin, the just ending of human life is eternal punishment, the logical outcome of humanity's inherent sinfulness, one which has alienated the human race from God and for which it deserves eternal punishment. Adam, in this sense, represents the whole of humanity. Propitiatory atonement, or the theory of penal substitution, is closely tied to this teaching.

The problem for us with predestination, as with propitiatory atonement, is that together they convey the idea that God needs something over and above what he is of himself (his sufficiency), or that he needs a supreme event to occur (which he then orchestrates in the sacrifice of his Son), in order to reverse human destiny. Both of these scenarios diminish God and restrict his freedom. They also suggest that there is some determining factor which makes certain people irredeemable, or that those who have been unlucky enough to land in the wrong Church may miss out on salvation because they do not hold the correct views about atonement and redemption, or of how God's grace works to that end. But when Christians are able to connect atonement and redemption with occasional glimpses of a transformed Church, and with the transformation of their own lives, they experience God's grace in knowing themselves to be a forgiven and redeemed people. This is the redemptive love of God at work, what I meant when I said in Chapter 1 that God becomes as we are, in order that we might become as he is.

In terms of concrete action, living as a forgiven people begins with forgiving ourselves (in allowing God to forgive us) and then continues in our forgiving of one another in the difficult business of reconciliation, especially where this concerns the truth and being faithful to Scripture. People are excluded from the Church's life on the basis of selective readings of Scripture which often serve to reinforce a single immovable understanding of truth, and therefore of God's love, and which marginalizes certain groups.

God's love, and therefore his truth, are also obscured by inhospitable and inflexible managerial structures and by a committee-driven approach to church life. Both of these foster a pragmatic legalism which diminishes the human person and inhibits the work of the Holy Spirit in the Church's mission. Jesus saw this general diminishment in the hypocrisy and petty legalism of the religious authorities of his time and it prompted a number of the angry exchanges which he had with them. He was angry because they used their power to exclude those who most needed God's love and because exclusive attitudes derail God's redemptive purpose for all people.

A hunger for holiness

What I have said so far about atonement and redemption suggests that God's redemptive purpose is revealed in a radical hospitality which is energized by a church's *spiritual* life. This ongoing receptivity to God's love is a dynamic activity and presents Christians with both a spiritual and a theological challenge, the two being closely related. Spiritually, churches often lack mystery. God has been domesticated, so as to make him appear 'relevant', and grace comes cheap. Many people who pass a church's door and then move on are actually seeking something less readily accessible. They would like less pre-packaged teaching, more silence, fewer easy answers and more acceptance of the fact that God does not always resolve suffering.[17]

Accepting God as he is, or letting God be God, is particularly important for those who suffer from depression and depression-related mental illness. It helps them to accept the present moment. It also relieves them of some of the pressure to be 'cured' the minute they start praying. One of the people I interviewed while preparing this book told me how important her

> **Letting God be God is particularly important for those who suffer from depression**

experience of Buddhism was to her in working out her Christian faith and in her spiritual journey. In exploring it within the context of her Christian prayer life, she finds that

> the practice of observing, accepting and being has been my lifeline in the worst times with my eating disorder, barrage of self-harming thoughts and depression. This is something that many parts of the Church neither know about, nor know how to minister with. I think it's a massive need, especially in the West where the pace, demands and busyness of life threatens to disconnect us all from our souls if we are not careful.

This indicates a great misunderstanding about the real significance of Christian prayer and the spiritual life for people today, many of whom never go near a church. There is a hunger for holiness, borne out by the fact that a growing number of books on spirituality of one kind or another are now on the market. The Church needs to actively engage with this need for holiness by promoting prayer. It ought to be a vital part of its work of mission and evangelism. But in order to do this, the Church will need to ensure that the spiritually gifted are selected for ordination (without, in the process, creating a spiritual elite) and given the preparation and training, and later the time, to walk alongside those who are struggling to know God better and to face the deep questions of faith. The same needs to be provided for gifted laity. This is because developing a deeper and more complex relationship with God is part of knowing what it means to have been justified by him, to have experienced his hospitality from the cross.

In equipping people for mission, the Church must help Christians rise to the secular challenges to religion in giving credible accounts of their faith. Prayer is the crucible in which faith is tested, refined and revealed to the world.[18] If the worshipping life of a group or church is to be more than an identity (charismatic, sacramental, traditional, etc.), prayer needs to become the energy which enlivens its mission by shaping the common life of its members in love and service to one another, and so enabling them to love and serve those around them. This suggests that faith grows with experiencing the redemptive love of God, God's grace, and that a community which is recognizably Christian is one in which all members welcome and celebrate diversity in the gifts and attributes of all its members, even those with whom they disagree or whom they dislike, because they discern God's love at work in them as well.[19] Ignoring the real person, and focusing only on certain criteria which qualify them for a particular church identity, blocks the activity of God's love in the common life of a church, so that everyone is the poorer.

Conclusion

Redemption is not a matter of choosing the right church or denomination, or of pre-determined fate, but of consciously choosing Jesus Christ, of laying hold of the love of God and of living from within his life. The ongoing work of redemption is an ongoing revelation of the meaning and purpose of human existence which is continually being worked out from within the risen life of Christ. In the final chapter of this book I shall be looking at how the redemption which has been wrought in the atoning work of the cross is only the beginning of that greater story.

6

If Christ is not risen

Did the resurrection really happen? Why was it
necessary? What does it have to do with the cross? What
kind of body did Jesus have when he rose again from
the dead? What does the resurrection of Christ mean
today?

What I have said so far in this book assumes that the reader accepts
Christ's suffering and death as a real event in history. The earliest
record we have of it (*circa* AD 91) is that of Josephus, a Jewish historian, who wrote that

> About this time arose Jesus, a wise man, who did good deeds and whose
> virtues were recognized. And many Jews and people of other nations
> became his disciples. Pilate condemned him to be crucified and to die.
> However, those who became his disciples preached his doctrine. They
> related that he had appeared to them three days after his crucifixion and
> that he was alive.[1]

The historian Tacitus referred to Christ's dying in a letter to the
emperor Trajan (AD 115) in which he describes the Christian community as followers of a 'pestilential superstition' which had grown
up around the memory of 'Christ[us] who had been executed in
Tiberius's time by the Procurator, Pontius Pilate'.[2] I hope to have
placed this apparently minor historical event within the greater
context of its significance for the human condition.

The life and death of Jesus Christ is a turning point in human
history. It represents an enduring reconciliation between God and
human beings in a re-orientation, or *metanoiea*, which God himself
initiates in his turning towards the human race. In the Old Testament
we often read of God 'repenting', or changing his mind, in relation
to a particular event or action.[3] In Christ he 'repents' in the hospitality
of the cross. He turns back and reclaims human beings from the

alienation of shame, the alienation which comes with not believing and trusting that God loves us and that his love is both enduring and all-sufficient.

Earlier, I said that the problem of sin has to do with a sundering of the trust which ought to exist between human beings and God. An emotionally healthy child does not question her parents' love because she has learned from an early age that her parents, and others, love her simply because she is worthy of their love. If sin has to do with a loss of confidence in our worthiness in God's eyes, it follows that it is also closely linked to fear of judgement and condemnation, and this fear makes it difficult for us to be vulnerable to receiving God's love. A person who cannot receive love cannot give it, or at least not without a great many years of painful life experience. Not being able to receive or give love is what Jesus called 'hardness of heart' and what I have called alienation.[4]

Hardness of heart begins with a feeling of unworthiness or shame. For Paul, it is fear of the law which causes sin in the first place, because a person is afraid of breaking it. For us, the law and legalism translate, in very general terms, as fear of those things which we imagine will expose our general unworthiness. We therefore live our lives in the fear of failure, of not conforming to our own, or to other people's, expectations. We live to protect our true selves from shame, and so we also live with disappoint-ment. These expectations vary from generation to generation but they fall under the general heading of what Paul calls the 'flesh', the mater-

> We live to protect our true selves from shame, so we live with disappointment

ial things or status symbols which make us feel worthy in our particular social context. Once we begin to feel a need for these material assets, we can never have enough of them, but they ultimately diminish and disempower us because they are in themselves lifeless. They absorb the person, and at the same time project a travesty of that person which can be used to manipulate or coerce others. Ultimately, our true personhood is reduced to a clone of that lifeless thing. This is a subject which is often explored metaphorically in science fiction films and books.[5]

There is no condemnation

The Gospel of John is written with a particular purpose in mind. John reveals each event in the life of Christ as a 'pointer' or 'sign' of who Christ is and of the purpose of his living and dying, which is to reclaim human beings for himself and, by inference, to give them back to themselves. The cross is the final act of God's absolute acceptance of the human condition and of every human person. In this moment of healing encounter, we are declared irrevocably to be worthy of God's love and, in accepting Christ, we begin to learn how to accept that love and to share it with one another.

Christ's dying is a decisive moment in human history in which judgement takes the form of mercy, rather than of condemnation. In his letter to the church at Rome, Paul says that 'There is therefore now no condemnation for those who are in Christ Jesus.'[6] The condemnation of which Paul speaks is the guilt and shame people carry about with them for being the kind of person they wrongly believe themselves to be, or for wrongs, or imagined wrongs, they may have done to others. But is there really a connection between this long-ago event and our own lives today? What difference can it make to the way we live our lives in the particular set of circumstances in which we find ourselves? Despite the horrific reality of the event itself, God's love still seems very abstract and the crucifixion of God's Son a world away from the humdrum realities of everyday life in the affluent West, if not of the suffering endured by millions elsewhere.

To begin to address these questions we need to remind ourselves of what it is that obscures the reality of the death of Christ from our view. There is a solid mass of 'matter' between us, the material and the selfish which literally hide God from our sight, and which, because of its distracting din, makes it impossible for us to hear his voice, his invitation to be reconciled and renewed. The exile metaphor which I used in the first chapter of this book was really about this situation which we have created for ourselves, or simply allowed to happen around us. It suggests two things. First, that the cross and the actual death of Christ cannot be the end of the story, since if he is simply dead he can no longer make his voice heard or reveal his presence with us, in any case. Second, that something still needs to happen which will break down whatever it is that goes on obscuring God from our sights, which goes on making it difficult for us to see him. Given that we exist in time and that human nature has not changed very much since the moment of Christ's death, it suggests that God in Jesus Christ needs to go on being present to us in a moving or dynamic way.

Enduring presence

Some Christians understand the Eucharist to be a repetition or a sacramental re-enactment of the sacrifice of the cross. Others, like Calvin, understand it as the activity of God's Holy Spirit, the very presence of Christ in the midst of those who are gathered together in his name, a presence which is not contingent on the words and actions of the celebrant but which 'waits upon' God's guests.[7] Both of these ways of thinking about the Eucharist affirm God's ongoing involvement with human beings which extends beyond the Eucharist itself. In the Eucharist, we experience the abiding and enduring presence of God's Spirit. Talking about the Holy Spirit as God's presence among us suggests that God's redemptive love is dynamic. It is first worked out in the atoning event of the cross, and it keeps pace with the lives which human beings are living now, in whatever circumstances or cultural context they find themselves. Jesus tells his disciples, shortly before his death, that 'A little while, and you will no longer see me, and again a little while, and you will see me.'[8] On another occasion, he promises, rather enigmatically, that in three days the temple of his body will be raised.[9] In both of these situations he wants to prepare his disciples for his death and resurrection. But in what sense did Christ rise from the dead? Why was it necessary? And if he did, is he still to be seen in the way his disciples and many hundreds of others saw him before his ascension to heaven?[10]

Risen and glorified

The idea of life after death was controversial, even in the first century. The ultra-conservative Sadducees, one of the two principal ruling parties of Judaism, did not believe in the possibility of someone continuing to live in some other dimension after death, let alone rising again physically from the grave. For us also, the physical resurrection of Christ defies logic. But it nevertheless reveals the fulfilment of Christ's purpose in coming to earth and the ultimate purpose of our own lives, that Christ be revealed in us so that we can be revealed in him.[11] His bodily resurrection is also promised to us as the consummation of human life, that human beings become a community of the resurrection with Christ as its head. But how is this resurrection to come about? What happens to people who have been cremated, or whose bodies have been mangled beyond recognition in war, or plane crashes, or road accidents?

The problem lies in the fact that we are thinking only in a single conceptual dimension, that the body which dies is the body which is raised on the last day. To some extent this is true, insofar as it is the person who is raised, but the body will be of a quite different order. Paul promises that 'what is sown is perishable, what is raised is imperishable'.[12] He is not saying that what is sown – a germ of wheat, for example – will be raised as something else – barley or olives perhaps. He is saying that the dead germ of wheat is raised as wheat which is completely renewed. It is literally 'a new creation'.[13] This is what we see in the resurrection of Jesus.

When the disciples first saw the Lord after he had risen, they either mistook him for someone else or just did not recognize him. But they did ultimately see him as the person they had always known. Mary recognizes him in the moment she hears her name called; the disciples on the Emmaus road begin to recognize him as he speaks to them about the things concerning him which were foretold in Scripture, and finally in the breaking of the bread. John and Peter recognize him in the context of fishing and the preparation of food on the beach. All of these situations speak of the recognition of faith, something which is known and understood in a single moment but which until now had been barely believed. All three of these examples have much to say about how human beings can still relate to the risen Christ. But for the moment I am concerned with what the disciples actually saw when they beheld the risen Jesus for the first time. They certainly did not see a bloody and mangled body, although one of them later touched the wounds in his hands and the scar left by the spear. The resurrection of Christ was not about reviving a man who was almost dead. Neither was it about the resuscitation of a corpse, but it did concern a body. Jesus ate and drank with the disciples. He was not simply an apparition which could later be written off as deluded fantasy on the part of his distraught followers. But what kind of body was it that they saw?

In many ways it would have been the same as the one they had known before the terrible events of the preceding few days, but it also pertained to another kind of existence, a redeemed existence. Piero della Francesca's painting of the risen Christ is, I think, the nearest we have to a visual representation of redeemed humanity. There is an energy in the figure of Christ which speaks of some profound and ultimate challenge that has been met and overcome. The face looks out and owns, or takes responsibility for, the viewer and the sleeping soldiers beside the tomb. It conveys a sovereignty which speaks of mercy and justice, but also of strength and peace. The risen Christ is revealed as what he is, fully human in his divinity and fully divine in his humanity, so that we, in our risen bodies, can expect to become fully what we are.

Becoming what we are

Atonement and redemption are consummated in the resurrection because it is in the resurrection that we are given back to ourselves. Because Christ is alive and still present to us, he is able to take us through the darkness of our own sin, the damage we do to ourselves and to others, and emerge with us into a new kind of future. Although the cross led to death, it also represents a doorway into a different kind of future, one which embodies hope.

Death is final. As with birth, it only happens once. Even allowing for near-death experiences, including recovering from a long-term coma, nobody really knows what it is like to exist in the context of eternity, in an altogether different dimension but one which also resonates with our own. Only Christ has experienced eternity, and what it is to be a self in that boundless and different time–space dimension, and afterwards returned fully alive in every sense. In his own risen body he invites us to contemplate the meaning of his resurrection for us, what it means to be entirely different and yet recognizably the same person for all of eternity.

It brings us back to the question I asked in the first chapter of this book: why atonement? I spoke of atonement as reconciliation with God effected in and through the death of Christ. This involves an active decision on the part of human beings to 'turn', to effect a *metanoiea* towards him and so receive grace and forgiveness, so that human beings can live together free of the guilt and shame which generates fear and leads to sin, or spiritual death. When we speak of the resurrection we begin to understand the implications of this freedom, not only for what we do but for who we are. The resurrection reveals what it means to become completely the persons God created us to be now, in this life, as well as in the next. In the resurrection, Christ transforms the human condition and human existence itself from what Paul calls 'futility' to one of endless potential for the bringing about of God's purpose in the world and in individual lives.

The word 'futility' is a particularly apt description of the vacuity and meaningless nature of the lives of many people today for whom the driving force is to succeed and to achieve. Failure and non-achievement amount to being a non-person, someone who has not been able to 'get a life' and use it for their own material betterment. But this reduction of life to the objective and material effects a corresponding diminishment of the individual's subjective personhood which depends on being alive in the fullest sense. Paul says that creation itself has also been subjected to futility and that God allowed this to happen 'in hope' so that it might one day share in the freedom of God's children.[14] The environmental disasters caused by human greed and irresponsible management are a sign of the earth's subjection to futility. They also reveal how its inner life, the life which is transcendent, or transparent to God, has been spoiled. Human beings have 'objectified' the earth by using and abusing it as a material asset to be plundered and exploited at will. The nineteenth-century poet Gerard Manley Hopkins speaks of the world's transcendence as that which 'is charged with the grandeur of God', of the way it has been spoiled by sin, and of the resulting human alienation from the earth:

Why do men then now not reck his rod?
Generations have trod, have trod, have trod;
And all is seared with trade; bleared, smeared with toil;
And wears man's smudge and shares man's smell: the soil
Is bare now, nor can foot feel, being shod.[15]

The resurrection of Christ sets the seal on the promise of covenant renewal, for the earth itself, and of renewal and reconciliation for all living things. It reveals transformation and so guarantees hope. All the encounters which Jesus has with his disciples after his resurrection reveal God's faithfulness to his promise. He allows men and women to begin again with God. In his book *Resurrection*, Rowan Williams speaks of the symbolism surrounding Christ's last days on earth which show the resurrection as a reconciliatory and renewing event. He describes how the fire which Jesus lights on the beach at the moment when Peter and John recognize the stranger on the shore corresponds to the fire which was lit in the outer courtyard of the temple and to Peter's denial of him there.[16] Here, we have the fire of renewed trust consuming the guilt and shame which Peter would have felt in the memory of his disloyalty on the night of the trial. Peter is being given the chance to become once again what he really is: not the disloyal coward but a friend who will be entrusted with the future of Christ's Church. Peter embodies the hope that comes with forgiveness and reconciliation. The Christian community is called to live that hope in its own relationships and in the secular world.

> **Peter is being given the chance to become once again what he really is**

Bearers of hope – living as forgiven people

Forgiveness and reconciliation are at the heart of redemption. They are a sign of the enduring presence of the risen Christ whose Holy Spirit is at work making new and meaningful connections in people's lives. These connections are discerned as part of the *metanoiea* process which is also ongoing, or dynamic, and are discerned in our remembering of the past.

Michael, a former alcoholic, told me how when he looked back on his life with all its wrong starts, broken relationships and failed attempts at dealing with his addiction, he saw, now that he had come back to his faith, that with God nothing is wasted. His life, including the hurt he had caused himself and others, was valuable to God. Michael realized that God had made a new creation out of the whole of that life, that nothing had been wasted, and that God was using it to enable him to minister to others from all that he had learned from those experiences.

The resurrection is about Christ's ongoing involvement with human beings. It is the outworking of atonement in ongoing redemption. For this to make sense, it helps to understand redemption not only as a once and for all event, but as God's continuing involvement with all human beings in the most profound, as well as the most trivial, moments of suffering. Redemption moves with the human condition and works in the ordinary and the everyday. Reconciliation, in whatever context and whatever form it takes, enables forward movement into something new. Michael's life was made new in the healing of his own broken past. This healing of the past can also happen in conflict resolution between nations, when one or other party is open to experiencing what it is to be the other person or the other group. A number of examples of this getting into the space of the other through the process of remembering have occurred in the fairly recent past.

The South African Truth and Reconciliation Commission, led by Archbishop Desmond Tutu, where people showed courage and generosity in speaking and hearing the truth about the suffering they had caused or endured, enabled the birth of a new nation. At the time of writing, we remain hopeful that the same will happen in Northern Ireland and that, one day, it may lead to an independent and autonomous Palestine. Already, there exists in Israel, and in the Jewish Diaspora, a growing number of people working together to take a stand against injustice and the dehumanizing effects of the occupation of Palestinian territory. The Jewish Voice for Peace seeks to redress some of the wrongs being committed in the name of Jews by lobbying for an end to the Israeli occupation of the West Bank, the Gaza Strip and East Jerusalem.[17] Of special significance is their desire to make Jerusalem a place of meeting between the three Abrahamic faiths, as well as between secular Palestinians and Israelis.[18] When this happens, Jerusalem will become a new creation, a visible sign of God's presence and of his redemptive work for the whole human race.

These stories are only approximate illustrations of what Paul meant when he challenged those who denied that Christ rose again after the Calvary event. He tells them that 'if Christ has not been raised, your faith is futile and you are still in your sins'.[19] In other words, the atoning work of the cross would not have differed from any other sacrificial offering. Without the new life which comes with his resurrection, and in which we share, it would have been a futile exercise. If there had been no resurrection, Christ would have simply died as a criminal outside the city walls, but he would never have met us inside the walls we build around ourselves and between one another, 'the walls of hostility'.

But if he rose again, as something more than an apparition – and here the word 'appeared', as it is used in the New Testament,[20] can be somewhat misleading[21] – he overcame not only death, but the finality of death. In doing so, he continues to invite human beings into a new state of existence with him now. Christ's cross and resurrection belong together as the ultimate sign of God's reconciling hospitality. If there was no resurrection, the cross and the death of Christ would remain remote from our own life experience. His death alone would not have reworked that experience into a new and dynamic way of living, as he does in the story told to me by Michael. It would not keep us moving towards one another in the renewal of our relationships. It would not allow us to explore what it means to be bound to Christ in life before death, as well as after it, so that our lives acquire meaning and purpose and our true identities are revealed to be more than signs of conformity to materialism and its various contextual agendas, whether secular or of the Church. The resurrection is the ultimate sign of God's faithfulness and of faith itself. So I would like to end this book with an example of how Christ's risen life and God's faithfulness is at work today and of how it is revealed in the faith of those who pray.

As I write, we are witnessing the rescue of 33 miners who have been trapped for nearly two months deep in the San José gold and copper mine near Copiapo, Chile. Their prolonged burial underground resonates with the burial of Christ and with his descent into hell, which we profess in our Creeds. But the men are also experiencing little moments of resurrection in the letters and messages they receive from family and friends who are waiting for them on the surface, in what has come to be known as the Camp of Hope. Resurrection and transformation are at work in the very small things which keep the men below alive, physically, spiritually and psychologically. These small gestures are the voice of the risen Christ calling their names. Little moments of resurrection are also changing lives and relationships on the surface. The waiting has brought out the truth, both for individuals and in family relationships. Sometimes the truth has been painful, but since the families are waiting

> **Little moments of resurrection are also changing lives and relationships**

and praying together to be reunited with those they love, their faith has helped to break down barriers and to strengthen their solidarity with one another. Truth and love are combining to strengthen faith. The trapped miners themselves are playing a prophetic role. Their situation challenges the greed and lack of concern for human life on the part of the mine's owners and investors, and it makes all of us think more about the real costs incurred by our use and abuse of the earth's mineral resources. The San José mine was known to be dangerous.

The miners and their rescuers, as well as their friends and families, are a sign of the ongoing redemptive work of the resurrection, of the existence of hope in the context of human relatedness. We see this same interplay between hope, faith and human relatedness in the resurrection event as it reconnects Jesus with his friends. When Mary Magdalen discovers that the stone which blocked the entrance to the tomb of the dead Christ has been rolled away, she experiences first anguish and anxiety, and then hope fulfilled, love affirmed and faith rewarded. The atonement and redemption which was wrought on the cross is made real, or fully revealed, when she hears Jesus calling her name. His call is the judgement of mercy, the same judgement we hear in testing situations in which forgiveness is at work. It is Christ calling our name, waiting for us to recognize him and become bearers of hope, sharers in the transforming work of a merciful and loving God.

Notes

1 Why atonement?

1 Anton Chekhov, *The Cherry Orchard* (Mineola, NY: Dover Publications, 1991), Act II.

2 *Oxford Dictionary*, ninth edition (Oxford: Oxford University Press, 2000).

3 In his novel *Riddley Walker*, Russell Hoban shows how, in the context of a post nuclear holocaust world of the future, a person's humanity is 'pared down' to a basic instinct for survival, and how the challenge to become human again is ultimately the key to the survival of the human race.

4 Francis Thompson, 'The Hound of Heaven', available at <http://www.houndsofheaven.com/thepoem.htm> (accessed 29 November 2010).

5 Throughout this book, where I use the word 'Church' I refer to the universal Church, or to a particular denomination within it, e.g. the Methodist Church. Where I use the word 'church' I am implying the local parish church, or church group.

6 David Tidmarsh argues that this basic sense of responsibility for another's well-being is learned in early childhood. It lays the foundation for a mature morality. It is also quite separate from the direct association of guilt with punishment; 'Necessary but not sufficient: the personal view of a psychiatric member of the parole board' in Murray Cox, ed., *Remorse and Reparation* (London: Jessica Kingsley, 1999), Chapter 3, pp. 49–50.

7 Joseph de Maistre (1753–1821) *Lettres et Opuscules Inédits*, vol. 1 (Paris: Vaton, 1861).

8 See Jurgen Moltmann, *The Crucified God* (London: SCM Press, 1974), Chapter 6. In this respect, Moltmann also draws our attention to the dangers of dwelling too heavily on God working in Christ alone, at the expense of the dynamic and reciprocal activity of the Trinity.

9 Drawing on the theology of the Cappadocian Fathers, Colin Gunton has argued that this dynamic or working love is a function of God's freedom. 'Relation and relativity: the Trinity and the created world' in Christoph Schwöbel, ed., *Trinitarian Theology Today*, Essays on Divine Being and Act series (Edinburgh: T&T Clark, 1995), p. 100.

10 We see God's impartial love and work of healing graphically portrayed in the context of the war in Afghanistan where the Red Cross trains Taliban soldiers in the basics of first aid. The Red Cross blog states that 'Under the Geneva Conventions the ICRC [The International Red Cross and Red

Crescent Movement] provides medical care for all people injured in a conflict, regardless of which side they're on – the armed forces are also bound by this and provide medical assistance to opposing combatants when possible': available at <http://blogs.redcross.org.uk/> (accessed 6 June 2010).

11 These formed part of what came to be known as the Holiness Code (Exod. 19—24) and ranged from the corruption of monotheistic worship to intermarriage with foreigners and the prohibition of incest and bestiality. Others were concerned with personal and food hygiene.

12 In his letter to the Galatians Paul wrestles with the question of the law which, although holy, is now redundant to these purposes. See Bruce W. Longenecker, *The Triumph of Abraham's God: The Transformation of Identity in Galatians* (Edinburgh: T&T Clark, 1998).

13 John 4.29.

14 John 8.2–11.

15 John 3.1–15.

16 Matt. 9.22.

17 Luke 18.38.

18 Phil. 2.7b–9.

19 As Jurgen Moltmann argues, this takes us beyond the idea of human obedience and faithfulness, but does not mean that in Christ's dying God ceases to exist. Similarly, Christ is more than an emissary or token. On the cross, he is fully revealed as the suffering God made man. See Moltmann, *The Crucified God*, Chapter 6, 'The crucified God'.

20 The Greek word *hinna* meaning 'in order that' is central to Paul's atonement theology. Morna Hooker builds this idea of interchange into the wider sense of our mutual belonging and participation in Christ. See *From Adam to Christ: Essays on Paul* (Cambridge: Cambridge University Press, 1990), Chapter 2, 'Interchange and atonement'.

2 The problem of sin

1 Rom. 3.20.

2 Richard Dawkins, *The Selfish Gene* (Oxford: Oxford University Press, 1978).

3 Daniel K. Brannan, 'Darwinism and original sin: Frederick R. Tennant's integration of Darwinian worldviews in Christian thought in the nineteenth century', *Journal for Interdisciplinary Research on Religion and Science*, No. 1 (July, 2007).

4 Gen. 3.5.

5 Gen. 3.24.

6 For a more detailed discussion of shame and guilt in relation to sin see Fraser Watts, 'Shame, sin and guilt' in Alistair McFadyen and Marcel Sarot, eds, *Forgiveness and Truth*, Explorations in Contemporary Theology series (London: T&T Clark, 2001).

7 *The Confessions of St Augustine* (London: Watkins Publishing, 2006), Book I:1.

8 Gen. 11.1–9.

9 'The spiritual repercussions of the atom bomb' in Pierre Teilhard de Chardin, *The Future of Man* (London: Collins, 1964), p. 144.

10 Rom. 7.21–25.

11 John 4.14.

12 For a fuller discussion of this approach to the problem of evil see Walter Wink, *Unmasking the Powers: The Invisible Forces that Determine Human Existence* (Philadelphia: Fortress Press, 1986), p. 167.

13 Wink, *Unmasking the Powers*, pp. 11ff.

14 As, for example, Gen. 6.6, Exod. 32.11–14 and 2 Sam. 24.16.

15 Matt. 13.4–9.

16 Rom. 8.28.

17 See Alistair McFadyen, *Bound to Sin: Abuse, Holocaust and the Christian Doctrine of Sin* (Cambridge: Cambridge University Press, 2000), Chapter 7, 'Power and participation: feminist theologies of sin', pp. 131ff.

18 Stephen Green, *Good Value: Reflections on Money, Morality and an Uncertain World* (London: Allen Lane, 2009).

3 The 'wrath' of God

1 John 14.6.

2 Terry Eagleton, *On Evil* (Yale: Yale University Press, 2010).

3 Augustine, *City of God* (Harmondsworth: Penguin Books, 2003), Book 12:1.

4 Rom. 7.21–25.

5 John Kabat-Zin, *Full Catastrophe Living: How to Cope with Stress, Pain and Illness Using Mindfulness Meditation* (London: Piatkus, 2004), especially Part IV.

6 This is 'the fear of the LORD' which is 'the beginning of wisdom'; Ps. 111.10 and Prov. 9.10.

7 Gal. 5.22–24. All of these belong intrinsically to the second of the two 'great commandments' given by Jesus himself, love of neighbour (Mark 12.31).

8 Certain Churches have emphasized humility as part of a 'submission' ethos. Others have encouraged women to model their lives on the Virgin Mary, who is romantically portrayed as a kind of feminine ideal.

9 Purity as an aspect of holiness has given rise, at certain periods in the Church's life, to a conditional and prohibitive approach to sinfulness, a 'thou shalt not' understanding of sin which, in certain church contexts, still leads to the exclusion of people on the basis of gender or sexuality. For a fuller discussion of how purity can damage the life of the Church see my *By One Spirit: Reconciliation and Renewal in Anglican Life* (London: Peter Lang, 2009), pp. 182–3.

10 For a discussion of the abuse of power in the Church see Martyn Percy, *Power and the Church: Ecclesiology in an Age of Transition* (London: Cassell, 1998), especially Chapter 4.

11 Not all scholars are agreed that Colossians is of Pauline authorship.

12 Christ becomes a curse in becoming what Jurgen Moltmann describes as 'the kind of person we don't want to be'; Jurgen Moltmann, *The Crucified God* (London: SCM Press, 1974), Chapter 6, p. 205.

13 Luke's Gospel, without the nativity and resurrection stories, was the only one of the four to survive in Marcion's revised canon. In their extensive editing of much of Paul's writing, he and his followers also added 'glosses' of their own to convey the impression that Paul was adamantly opposed to the God portrayed in the rabbinical tradition.

14 We should note, in this respect, that the goat represents the community but is not a substitute for it.

15 Gen. 9.4.

16 Eph. 2.14.

17 In the book of Isaiah religious decadence brings about the fall of the northern kingdom of Israel. The folly of its leaders is the result of a religious syncretism which clouds their political judgement and undermines their trust in God.

18 For a fuller discussion of the subjective and objective nature of God's love see Paul Fiddes, *Past Event and Present Salvation: The Christian Idea of Atonement* (London: Darton, Longman and Todd, 1989), pp. 26ff.

19 John 1.5.

20 See R. V. G. Tasker, 'The biblical doctrine of the wrath of God', reproduced in D. E. H. Whitley, *The Theology of St Paul* (Oxford: Blackwell, 1974), p. 62.

21 Stated in more prosaic terms, God's love has the effect on the guilt and shame experienced through sin that bleach has on a stain. In God's eyes, it is as if the stain had never been. See Morna Hooker, *From Adam to Christ: Essays on Paul* (Cambridge: Cambridge University Press, 1990), Part I, 'Interchange in Christ'.

22 Julian of Norwich, *Revelations of Divine Love* (Harmondsworth: Penguin Classics, 1998), Chapter 29. In much of her writing, Julian struggles to

remain within the bounds of the Catholic Church's teaching, so there is often considerable disparity in her thinking within a single chapter, but she returns invariably to the love of God shown on the cross.

23 2 Cor. 5.21. Paul uses the Greek phrase *hinna*, meaning 'in order that', to explain that aspect of expiatory atonement which has become known as 'interchange'; see Hooker, *From Adam to Christ*, Chapter 1.

24 Deut. 10.17–18; cf. Exod. 22.21–24.

25 Deut. 10.17–18; cf. Exod. 22.21–24.

26 John 1.29.

27 Rom. 8.1.

28 A number of prisons in the UK are now allowing prisoners to meet with their victims in a controlled environment. The process is known internally as 'the sorry course'.

29 For a fuller discussion of the relationship between the psychological and theological implications of forgiveness see Deborah van Deusen Hunsinger, 'Forgiving abusive parents' in Alistair McFadyen *et al.*, eds, *Forgiveness and Truth: Explorations in Contemporary Theology* (Edinburgh: T&T Clark, 2001), pp. 71ff.

30 John 20.23. Jesus gives his disciples the authority to forgive or to retain sins, but it is not a way of conferring power.

31 Col. 1.20.

32 Rev. 22.2.

4 The redemptive love of God

1 Isa. 44.1; John 15.16.

2 Ps. 22.1; Matt. 27.46; cf. Isa. 49.14.

3 Rom. 5.8.

4 John 1.5; and see p. 41.

5 Mark 15.39.

6 Ps. 119.34.

7 Job 19.25.

8 For a comprehensive discussion of how the Church's life is becoming increasingly secularized, see Robin Greenwood, *Transforming Church: Liberating Structures for Ministry* (London: SPCK, 2002), especially Chapter 1.

9 Daniel Hardy describes this as a gradual revelation and practical outworking of a collective desire for the good. 'This implies the closest relation between historically contingent life and goodness, that historical life is a yearning for the good embodied in incremental steps toward it'; 'Goodness in history' in Daniel Hardy, *Finding the Church: The Dynamic Truth of Anglicanism* (London: SCM Press, 2001), p. 69.

10 'Because you're worth it' is the tag line of a cosmetic brand.

11 For a penetrating discussion of the relationship between freedom, choice and relationships, see Rowan Williams, *Lost Icons: Reflections on Cultural Bereavement* (Edinburgh: T&T Clark, 2000), Chapter 1.

12 He describes a situation in which 'The one strives to draw into itself everything that surrounds it, ensnaring it in its own life and, wherever possible, absorbing it into its innermost being. The other longs to extend its own inner self ever further, thereby permeating and imparting to everything from within, while never being exhausted itself'; Friedrich Schleiermacher, 'First speech' in his *On Religion: Speeches to its Cultured Despisers*, ed. and trans. Richard Crouter, Cambridge Texts in the History of Philosophy series (Cambridge: Cambridge University Press, 2008), p. 5.

13 Gal. 5.1.

14 Augustine, *Confessions*, trans. Henry Chadwick (Oxford: Oxford University Press, 1991), Book 1:1(i).

15 'Faith is the state of being grasped by the power of being itself'; Paul Tillich, *The Courage to Be* (London: Collins Fontana Library, 1964), p. 167.

16 Jesus speaks of the ongoing creative process at work in his own creative life of obedience to the Father; John 5.17.

17 2 Cor. 5.19.

18 This should not be confused with the highly contentious idea of *Patripassianism*, originally proposed by the second-century theologian Praxias (and contested by Tertullian), who argued that God the Father suffered and was crucified with his Son.

19 This is not to deny that God's redemptive work is going on in the context of other faiths, or to underestimate the destabilizing effect on the world and society of turning any one faith into an exclusive and excluding ideology. For an extended and insightful discussion of the wider faith issues raised by the redemptive work of Christ, in relation to Judaism in particular, see Rowan Williams, 'The finality of Christ' in his *On Christian Theology*, Challenges in Contemporary Theology series (Oxford: Blackwell, 2000), Chapter 7.

20 Luke 15.11–32.

21 Bernard of Clairvaux, *Opera Omnia*, ed. Jean Leclercq, Charles H. Talbot and Henri Rochais (Rome: Editiones Cistercienses, 1957–78), Homily 4: 8–9.

22 John 4.7–26.

5 Ongoing redemption

1 See Chapter 1, note 5.

2 Gal. 5.1.

3 Robin Greenwood describes this as an ongoing 'reactive round' designed to maintain the existing Church's status quo. See his *Transforming Church: Liberating Structures for Ministry* (London: SPCK, 2002), Chapter 1, p. 8.

4 Quoted in Philip Richter and Leslie Francis, *Gone but Not Forgotten: Church Leaving and Returning* (London: Darton, Longman and Todd, 1998).

5 George Herbert, 'Love', available at <http://www.poetry-archive.com/h/love.html> (accessed 29 November 2010).

6 The Bible is itself Salvation History, an account of the way God works both with and for human beings in a continual invitation to join with him in his ongoing creative purpose for the world.

7 2 Cor. 6.14.

8 With the growth of the Christian Union in universities and institutes of higher education, people from other denominations are now defining themselves as 'Christian' by way of signalling a shared commitment to Christ.

9 These two do not automatically go together. There is, for example, a surprising amount of antipathy to women's ministry among gay clergy in certain Provinces of the Anglican Communion.

10 A double backlash against controlling and systemic thinking in the Church is developing in the USA today. It signals a growing resistance to unchecked fundamentalism and a growing disillusionment at the institutionalization of the Church. Almost one-third of Americans today are unchurched Christians. See Harriet Barber, 'Missing the good of churchgoing', *Church Times*, 17 September 2010.

11 The recent revelations of the sexual abuse of children by Catholic priests has exacerbated the distrust of clergy in general, although it is also opening up a long overdue debate concerning the real significance and purpose, if any, of priestly celibacy.

12 1 John 4.18.

13 See Daniel W. Hardy, 'The Sociality of Evangelical Catholicity' in *Finding the Church* (London: SCM Press, 2001).

14 For more on this, see below (p. 71).

15 Rom. 12.9.

16 Space does not permit the great deal more which remains to be said on this subject, including the subtle interfacing of predestination between the teaching of Augustine and that of Aquinas.

17 This point is well made by Monica Furlong in the introduction to her book, *C of E: The State It's In*, second edition (London: SPCK, 2006).

18 Some of its detractors confuse faith and prayer with a comforting and naive belief in a God who they expect to behave like a fairy godmother.

In one of his numerous indictments of Christian prayer, Christopher Hitchens states that 'We pray sincerely, knowing that when God answers this completely heartfelt, unselfish, non-materialistic prayer, it will glorify God and help millions of people in remarkable ways. Will anything happen? No. Of course not'; <http://godisimaginary.com/i1.htm> (accessed 15 September 2010).

19 Brad Harper and Paul Louis Metzger, *Exploring Ecclesiology: An Evangelical and Ecumenical Introduction* (Grand Rapids, MN: Brazos Press, 2009), Chapter 2.

6 If Christ is not risen

1 *Jewish Antiquities* XVIII 3:2; available at <http://classics.mit.edu/Josephus/j.aj.html> (accessed 29 November 2010).

2 Tacitus, *Annals*, XV 44; available at <http://classics.mit.edu/Tacitus/annals.html> (accessed 29 November 2010).

3 He repents of having made Saul king (1 Sam. 15.35). The Lord's repenting is also synonymous with his mercy (Jer. 31.20). See also Amos 7.3–6 and Zech. 8.14.

4 Matt. 19.8; Mark 3.5. He uses this expression to reveal what is really at stake in dysfunctional marriages as well as human indifference to suffering.

5 Two episodes of *Doctor Who* (BBC Wales, 2005) have treated the subject in different ways. In the first, the Autons make a plastic double of Mickey, Rose's boyfriend, in order to attack the Doctor. In the second, the Slitheens disguise themselves as humans and attack 10 Downing Street, where they reveal their true personas by peeling off their borrowed 'human' skins.

6 Rom. 8.1.

7 For a comprehensive account of Calvin's eucharistic theology see B. A. Gerrish, *Grace and Gratitude: The Eucharistic Theology of John Calvin* (Edinburgh: T&T Clark, 1993).

8 John 16.16.

9 John 2.18–22.

10 Acts 1.3.

11 Col. 3.4.

12 1 Cor. 15.42.

13 2 Cor. 5.17.

14 Rom. 8.20–21.

15 Gerard Manley Hopkins, 'God's Grandeur'; <http://www.bartleby.com/122/7.html> (accessed 29 November 2010).

16 Rowan Williams, *Resurrection: Interpreting the Easter Gospel* (London: Darton, Longman and Todd, 2002), pp. 28ff.

17 Jewish Voice for Peace can be accessed at <http://www.jewishvoiceforpeace.org/content/jvp-mission-statement> (accessed 29 November 2010).

18 Hello Peace! is another sign of reconciliation and new life in the Middle East. This is a coordinated telephoning exercise aimed at promoting greater understanding between Palestinians and Israelis and between the three Abrahamic faiths; <http://traubman.igc.org/call-now.htm> (accessed 29 November 2010).

19 1 Cor. 15.17.

20 Luke 24.34; Acts 9.17, 26.16.

21 See Dave Tomlinson, *Re-Enchanting Christianity: Faith in an Emerging Culture* (Norwich: Canterbury Press, 2008), Chapter 8, p. 71.

Further reading

Augustine, *Confessions*, trans. Henry Chadwick, The World's Classics (Oxford: Oxford University Press, 1991).

Cavanagh, Lorraine, *By One Spirit: Reconciliation and Renewal in Anglican Life* (Oxford: Peter Lang, 2009).

Chadwick, Owen, *The Reformation*, Penguin History of the Church vol. 3 (Harmondsworth: Penguin Books, 1972).

Cox, Murray, ed., *Remorse and Reparation*, Forensic Focus 7 (London: Jessica Kingsley Publishers, 1999).

Dell, Katherine, *Shaking a Fist at God: Understanding Suffering Through the Book of Job* (London: Fount Paperbacks, 1995).

Dillistone, F. W., *The Christian Understanding of Atonement* (Welwyn: James Nisbet, 1968).

Eagleton, Terry, *On Evil* (Yale: Yale University Press, 2010).

Fiddes, Paul S., *Past Event and Present Salvation: The Christian Idea of Atonement* (London: Darton, Longman and Todd, 1989).

Finlan, Stephen, *Problems with Atonement: The Origins of, and Controversy about, the Atonement Doctrine* (Collegeville, Minnesota: Liturgical Press, 2005).

Hauerwas, Stanley and Willimon, William H., *Resident Aliens* (Nashville: Abingdon Press, 1989).

Holloway, Richard, *On Forgiveness* (Edinburgh: Canongate Books, 2002).

Hooker, Morna D., *From Adam to Christ: Essays on Paul* (Cambridge: Cambridge University Press, 1990).

Kimball, Dan, *They Like Jesus but Not the Church: Insights from Emerging Generations* (Grand Rapids, Michigan: Zondervan, 2007).

McFadyen, Alistair, *Bound to Sin: Abuse, Holocaust and the Christian Doctrine of Sin*, Cambridge Studies in Christian Doctrine (Cambridge: Cambridge University Press, 2000).

McFadyen, Alistair, Sarot, Marcel and Thiselton, Anthony, eds, *Forgiveness and Truth: Explorations in Contemporary Theology*, The Society for the Study of Theology: Explorations in Contemporary Theology (Edinburgh: T&T Clark, 2001).

McLaren, Brian, *A Generous Orthodoxy* (Grand Rapids, Michigan: Zondervan, 2004).

Moltmann, Jurgen, *The Crucified God* (London: SCM Press, 1974).

Moltmann, Jurgen, *Jesus Christ for Today's World*, trans. Margaret Kohl (London: SCM Press, 1994).

Pattison, Stephen, *Shame: Theory, Therapy, Theology* (Cambridge: Cambridge University Press, 2000).

Sacks, Jonathan, *To Heal a Fractured World: The Ethics of Responsibility* (London: Continuum, 2005).

Tillich, Paul, *The Courage to Be* (London: Fontana Library, 1952).

Tomlinson, Dave, *Re-Enchanting Christianity: Faith in an Emerging Culture* (Norwich: Canterbury Press, 2008).

Tutu, Desmond, *God Has a Dream: A Vision of Hope for Our Time* (London and Johannesburg: Rider, 2005).

Volf, Miroslav, *Exclusion and Embrace: A Theological Exploration of Identity, Otherness and Reconciliation* (Nashville: Abingdon Press, 1996).

Williams, H. A., *True Resurrection* (London: Collins Fount, 1983).

Williams, Rowan, *Resurrection: Interpreting the Easter Gospel* (London: Darton, Longman and Todd, 2002 edition).

Wink, Walter, *Unmasking the Powers: The Invisible Forces that Determine Human Existence* (Philadelphia: Fortress Press, 1986).